COMPUTER
ARCHITI
AN
ORGANIZATION

B. Lalithadevi | P. Nandhini | T. Bhanu Shree | K. Triveni

KHANNA BOOK
PUBLISHING CO. (P) Ltd.
4C/4344, Ansari Road, Darya Ganj,
New Delhi, India

Sathyabama Institute of
Science and Technology
Jeppiaar Nagar, Rajiv Gandhi Salai,
Chennai, Tamilnadu, India

Dear Readers,

To prevent the piracy, this book is secured with HIGH SECURITY HOLOGRAM on the front title cover. In case you don't find the hologram on the front cover title, please write us to at contact@khannabooks.com or whatsapp us at +91-99109 09320 and avail special gift voucher for yourself.

Specimen of Hologram on front Cover title:

Moreover, there is a SPECIAL DISCOUNT COUPON for you with EVERY HOLOGRAM.

How to avail this SPECIAL DISCOUNT:

Step 1: Scratch the hologram
Step 2: Under the scratch area, your "coupon code" is available
Step 3: Logon to www.khannabooks.com
Step 4: Use your "coupon code" in the shopping cart and get your copy at a special discount
Step 5: Enjoy your reading!

Thanks,
Khanna Publishing House

ISBN: 978-93-55388-03-2

COMPUTER ARCHITECTURE AND ORGANIZATION

by **B. Lalithadevi | P. Nandhini**
T. Bhanu Shree | K. Triveni

First Edition: 2025

To view complete list of books, please scan the QR Code:

Published by:
Khanna Book Publishing Co. (P) Ltd.
CIN: U22110DL1998PTC095547

Visit us at: www.khannabooks.com
Write us at: contact@khannabooks.com

Printed in Bharat.

Preface

Computers play a vital role in modern technology, enabling advancements in various fields such as communication, healthcare, and artificial intelligence. Understanding how computers work internally is essential for designing efficient and high-performance systems. This book provides a structured approach to learning Computer Architecture and Organization, covering fundamental concepts that define the operation of computing systems.

The book begins with an introduction to the basic components of a computer, including registers, instruction processing, and system organization. It explains how data is stored, retrieved, and processed, laying the foundation for understanding complex computing operations. The discussion includes instruction cycles, stack organization, and the role of different types of registers in execution.

Further, the book explores arithmetic and logic operations, memory organization, and input-output mechanisms. It describes how processors perform mathematical and logical computations, how different types of memory enhance performance, and how computers communicate with external devices. Concepts such as memory hierarchy, cache memory, and direct memory access (DMA) are explained in a clear and concise manner.

Multiprocessing and parallel computing are becoming increasingly important in modern computing. The book introduces interconnection structures, interprocessor communication, and synchronization techniques used in multiprocessor systems. It also covers cache coherence mechanisms that ensure data consistency across multiple processors.

Designed for students and professionals, this book balances theoretical concepts with practical applications. Each topic is presented in a structured manner with clear explanations and real-world examples. By the end of this book, readers will gain a strong understanding of Computer Architecture and Organization, preparing them for advanced studies and careers in computing technology.

Contents

General Registers

UNIT 1

RATIONALE

Understanding general registers and basic computer organization is essential for grasping how processors execute instructions and manage data efficiently. Registers serve as high-speed storage within the CPU, reducing memory access time and improving execution speed. The study of stack organization, instruction formats, and computer registers lays the foundation for understanding instruction execution, data manipulation, and memory hierarchy. These concepts are crucial for optimizing processor performance, designing efficient computing systems, and enhancing problem-solving capabilities in computer architecture.

OUTCOMES

This unit provides an understanding of general register organization, stack organization, and the fundamentals of basic computer architecture. It covers different instruction codes, computer registers, and the instruction cycle. By the end of this unit, students will:

- Understand the structure and role of general registers in a computer system.
- Learn the significance of stack organization in execution control and function calls.
- Identify various types of instruction codes and their implementation.
- Differentiate between different types of computer registers and their functions.
- Analyze the instruction cycle, including fetching, decoding, and execution processes.
- Gain insights into basic computer organization and its functional components.

1.1 Introduction

Understanding computer architecture involves examining key components, including the role of general registers within the Central Processing Unit (CPU). The CPU serves as the core processing unit of a computer, executing instructions in a sequence of fetching, decoding, executing, and storing operations. Registers within the CPU function as high-speed storage locations, temporarily holding data during computation. These registers are classified as general-purpose registers (GPRs) and

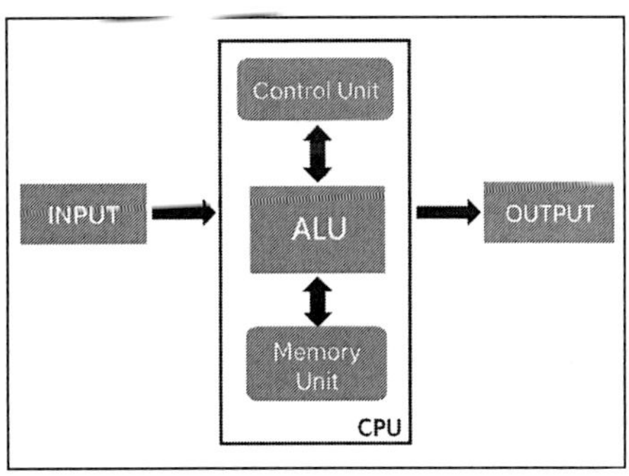

Fig 1.1: Components of the CPU

special-purpose registers, where GPRs are utilized for arithmetic operations, temporary storage, data transfer, and addressing. The CPU consists of the following major components:

- Control Unit (CU)
- Arithmetic Logic Unit (ALU)
- Memory or Storage Unit

1. Control Unit (CU)

The Control Unit functions as the operational hub of the CPU, directing the execution of instructions. It is responsible for managing the flow of data between the processor and memory.

Functions of the Control Unit

- **Instruction Fetching:** Retrieves instructions from Random Access Memory (RAM).
- **Instruction Decoding:** Interprets the fetched instructions.
- **Instruction Execution:** Sends control signals to perform arithmetic and logical operations through the ALU.
- **Control Flow Management:** Maintains the sequence of execution by updating the program counter.
- **Exception Handling:** Manages errors, system calls, and external interruptions by redirecting control flow.
- **Synchronization:** Coordinates multi-core execution.

2. Arithmetic Logic Unit (ALU)

The Arithmetic Logic Unit (ALU) is a highly optimized component responsible for executing arithmetic and logical operations. It operates in conjunction with CPU registers, memory, and the control unit.

Functions of the ALU

- **Arithmetic Operations:** Performs fundamental operations such as addition, subtraction, multiplication, and division.
- **Logical Operations:** Executes bitwise operations, including AND, OR, NOT, XOR, and bit-shifting.

3. Memory Unit

The memory unit is a crucial component used to store and retrieve data as needed. Computer memory is broadly categorized into:

1. **Primary Memory (RAM):** Volatile storage used for active program execution.
2. **Secondary Memory (Hard Disk, SSD):** Non-volatile storage for long-term data retention.

Functions of Primary Memory

- Acts as temporary storage for active programs and instructions.
- Loses stored data when the computer is turned off.

- Holds essential system files and software for smooth operations.
- Enhances multitasking and execution speed based on available capacity.

Functions of the CPU

The primary functions of the CPU include:

- Performing arithmetic and logical operations.
- Directing processing tasks.
- Managing input and output unit operations.
- Temporarily storing data within registers.
- Executing instructions retrieved from memory.

1.2 General Register Organization

Registers within the CPU are designed for high-speed data processing and temporary storage of critical information. Registers reduce memory access time and enhance execution speed.

Key Functions of Registers

- **Temporary Data Storage:** Enables rapid access to frequently used data.
- **Instruction Execution:** Holds instructions during processing.
- **Status Retention:** Maintains information about active processes and execution status.

Types of CPU Registers

- **Data Register (DR):** Stores operands and computation results.
- **Address Register (AR):** Holds memory addresses for operations.
- **Accumulator (AC):** Stores intermediate computation outcomes.
- **Instruction Register (IR):** Contains the current instruction being processed.
- **Program Counter (PC):** Tracks the next instruction in sequence.
- **Temporary Register (TR):** Holds temporary data during execution.

Bus System and Data Flow in the CPU

The CPU bus system, managed by the control unit, directs data flow through the ALU by selecting the appropriate operations and components. A basic computational instruction, such as $R1 \leftarrow R2 + R3$, involves the following CPU functions:

Operations in the CPU

- **MUX A Selector (SELA):** Transfers R2 into Bus A.
- **MUX B Selector (SELB):** Transfers R3 into Bus B.
- **ALU Operation Selector (OPR):** Selects and executes the addition operation.
- **Decoder Destination Selector (SELD):** Stores the result in R1.

Register Addressing and Micro-Operations

The CPU employs micro-operations to execute arithmetic and logical tasks efficiently. The following examples illustrate micro-operations:

Example Instruction

MULT R1, R2, R3

This multiplication instruction involves three registers.

The operation can also be simplified as **MULT R1, R2**, where R1 stores the final product.

Table 1.1: *Encoding of Register Selection Fields*

Binary Code	SELA	SELB	SELD
000	Input	Input	None
001	R1	R1	R1
010	R2	R2	R2
011	R3	R3	R3
100	R4	R4	R4
101	R5	R5	R5
110	R6	R6	R6
111	R7	R7	R7

ALU Micro-Operations and Execution

Micro-operations are essential for efficient CPU functioning.

Some common ALU operations are outlined below:

Table 1.2: *Encoding of ALU Operations:*

OPR Select	Operation	Symbol
00000	Transfer A	TSFA
00001	Increment A	INCA
00010	Add A + B	ADD
00101	Subtract A - B	SUB
00110	Decrement A	DECA
01000	AND A and B	AND
01010	OR A and B	OR
01100	XOR A and B	XOR
01110	Complement A	COMA
10000	Shift right A	SHRA
11000	Shift left A	SHLA

Understanding general register organization is essential for optimizing CPU performance. Efficient register utilization minimizes memory dependency, reduces execution time, and enhances overall computing efficiency. Future advancements in processor design will continue to refine register architectures, improving speed and processing capability in modern computing systems.

1.3 Stack Organization

A stack is an essential memory structure in computer architecture that follows the Last In, First Out (LIFO) principle. This means that the last data element stored is the first one to be retrieved. Stacks play a crucial role in memory management, function calls, and arithmetic operations within the Central Processing Unit (CPU). The stack is implemented using a Stack Pointer (SP), which keeps track of the topmost element in the stack.

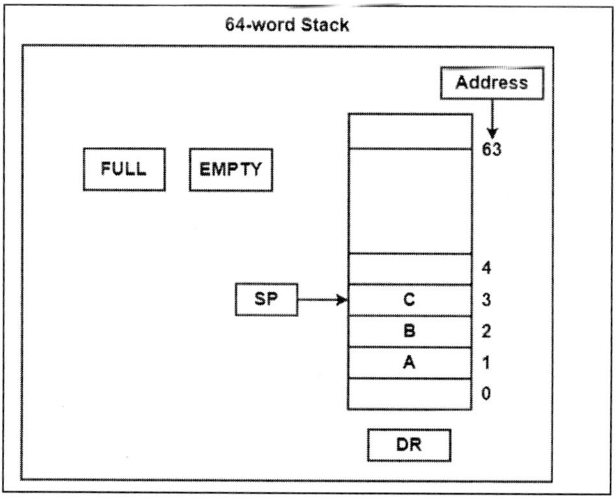

Fig 1.2: Representation of stack organization

Stack Operations

The stack operates through two fundamental operations:

1. **Push:** Adds an element to the top of the stack.
2. **Pop:** Removes the top element from the stack.

These operations manipulate the Stack Pointer (SP), which adjusts accordingly to track the stack's top position.

Register Stack

A register stack consists of high-speed memory locations that temporarily store values during execution. This enhances processing efficiency by reducing frequent accesses to main memory. Consider a 64-word register stack, where the stack pointer keeps track of the most recently added element.

- Suppose the stack holds three elements: A, B, and C.
- **C is the top element,** and its address is stored in SP.
- **When POP is executed,** C is removed, and SP updates to point to B.
- **When PUSH is executed,** a new element is added, and SP moves to the next available position.

Stack Pointer Register

The Stack Pointer (SP) is a specialized register that holds the address of the **top element** in the stack. The stack typically operates within a fixed address range in memory.

- **When the stack is full**, the **FULL flag** is set to 1.
- **When the stack is empty**, the **EMPTY flag** is set to 1.
- SP is updated dynamically based on stack operations.
- Stack Implementation and Micro-Operations

Push Operation

- Increment SP → SP ← SP + 1
- Store new element → Memory[SP] ← DR
- If SP reaches the stack limit, set **FULL flag**
- Mark **EMPTY flag** as 0

Pop Operation

- Retrieve element → DR ← Memory[SP]
- Decrement SP → SP ← SP - 1
- If SP reaches 0, set **EMPTY flag**
- Mark **FULL flag** as 0

Memory Stack

A **memory stack** is a portion of RAM reserved for stack operations. Unlike register stacks, memory stacks operate within the computer's main memory. This is typically divided into three sections:

- **Program Instructions:** Stores executable instructions.
- **Data Section:** Holds program variables.
- **Stack Section:** Manages function calls and data storage.

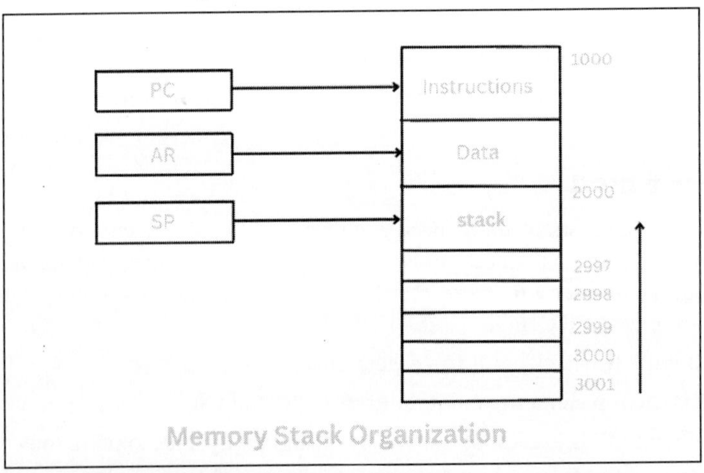

Fig 1.3: Representation of memory stack organization

Stack Growth Direction

The stack can grow in two directions:

- **Upward Stack:** Stack Pointer increments when data is pushed.

- **Downward Stack:** Stack Pointer decrements when data is pushed.

Most architectures use a downward-growing stack, where memory addresses decrease as new elements are added.

Stack Registers and Addressing

The CPU manages stack operations using the following registers:

- **Program Counter (PC):** Holds the address of the next instruction.
- **Address Register (AR):** Points to the location of the required data.
- **Stack Pointer (SP):** Tracks the top of the stack.

Example of Stack Operations

1. Push Operation Example

Before PUSH

SP = 3001

Stack = {10, 20, 30}

Executing PUSH(40)

SP = 3000

Stack = {10, 20, 30, 40}

2. Pop Operation Example

Before POP

SP = 3000

Stack = {10, 20, 30, 40}

Executing POP

SP = 3001

Stack = {10, 20, 30}

Stack organization is fundamental to **efficient CPU operation** and memory management. It facilitates recursive function calls, expression evaluations, and interrupt handling. Understanding how the stack operates through **Push and Pop operations** helps in designing efficient computing architectures. Future improvements in stack organization will continue to enhance processing speed and resource optimization.

1.4 Basic Computer Organization

Computer organization defines the structural framework and interconnections of various hardware components that enable a computer to function efficiently. It focuses on how different units of a computer system collaborate to process and execute instructions seamlessly.

Components of a Computer System

- **Central Processing Unit (CPU):** The **CPU** is the primary component responsible for executing instructions and processing data. It consists of:

- **Control Unit (CU):** Manages and coordinates the execution of instructions by interpreting them and directing system operations.
- **Arithmetic Logic Unit (ALU):** Conducts arithmetic computations and logical operations.
- **Registers:** High-speed storage units for temporarily holding data and instructions during processing.
- **Memory Unit:** The memory unit is essential for storing and retrieving data and instructions for execution. It includes:
- **Primary Memory:** Comprises **RAM** (volatile memory used for temporary data storage) and **ROM** (non-volatile memory storing essential firmware instructions).
- **Secondary Memory:** Consists of permanent storage solutions such as hard disk drives (HDDs) and solid-state drives (SSDs) for long-term data retention.

Bus Architecture

A **bus** serves as the communication channel that facilitates data transfer between various computer components. The three primary types of buses include:

- **Data Bus:** Transmits actual data between different components.
- **Address Bus:** Carries memory addresses to specify the location of data.
- **Control Bus:** Transfers control signals to regulate and synchronize operations across the system.

Input/Output (I/O) System

The **I/O system** allows interaction between the computer and external devices, enabling data input and output processes.

- **Input Devices:** Examples include keyboards, mice, scanners, and microphones.
- **Output Devices:** Examples include monitors, printers, and speakers.
- **I/O Interfaces:** Act as communication bridges between the CPU and peripherals to ensure seamless data transfer.

Memory Hierarchy

Memory in a computer system is structured in a hierarchy to optimize access speed and efficiency while balancing cost:

- **Registers:** The fastest and smallest memory, directly integrated into the CPU.
- **Cache Memory:** A small, high-speed storage area that stores frequently accessed data to enhance processing speed.
- **Main Memory (RAM):** A larger but slower memory used for temporary data storage during program execution.
- **Secondary Storage:** Non-volatile storage, such as HDDs and SSDs, used for long-term data retention and backup.

Instruction Cycle

The **instruction cycle** describes the sequence of operations performed by the CPU to process an instruction. It includes the following steps:

1. **Fetch:** The CPU retrieves the instruction from memory.
2. **Decode:** The instruction is analyzed and interpreted.
3. **Execute:** The required operation is performed.
4. **Store:** The result is written back to memory or a register.

Basic Input/Output System (BIOS)

The **BIOS** is a crucial firmware component responsible for hardware initialization and system startup.

- **Function:** Conducts system diagnostics (POST), loads the bootloader, and manages hardware configurations.
- **Components:** Stored in ROM and executed immediately upon powering the system.

Motherboard

The **motherboard** serves as the primary circuit board interconnecting the CPU, memory, and peripherals. It provides the essential framework and pathways for data communication across all hardware components.

Performance Considerations

The performance of a computer system is influenced by various factors, including:

Clock Speed: Measured in GHz, determines the number of instructions the CPU can execute per second.

- **Cores and Threads:** Multi-core processors allow parallel execution of multiple tasks, improving performance and multitasking capabilities.
- **Cache Size:** Larger caches store frequently accessed data closer to the CPU, reducing retrieval time and enhancing efficiency.
- **RAM Capacity:** A greater amount of RAM allows more applications to run simultaneously without slowing down the system.
- **Bus Speed:** Faster buses enhance data transfer rates between the CPU, memory, and peripherals.

1.5 Instruction Codes and Formats

Instruction codes are fundamental machine language commands that a processor interprets and executes. These instructions dictate how a computer processes data and performs various tasks. Each instruction consists of multiple fields, including:

- **Opcode (Operation Code):** Defines the operation to be executed.
- **Address Field:** Specifies the location of the operand in memory or register.
- **Mode Field:** Determines how the operand is accessed.

Types of Instruction Codes

A basic computer utilizes three primary instruction code formats:

- **Memory-Reference Instructions:** Uses memory locations for operand storage, with 12 bits allocated for addressing and one bit for the addressing mode.

- **Register-Reference Instructions:** Identified by an opcode of 111 and a 0 in bit 15, these instructions operate directly on the Accumulator (AC) register.
- **Input-Output Instructions:** Similar to register-reference instructions but have a 1 in bit 15, specifying I/O operations without needing memory references.

Instruction Set Completeness

A well-defined instruction set should include:

- **Arithmetic, Logical, and Shift Instructions:** Enables numerical calculations and logical evaluations.
- **Data Transfer Instructions:** Allows data movement between memory and processor registers.
- **Program Control Instructions:** Includes branching and conditional instructions for managing execution flow.
- **Input and Output Instructions:** Handles data exchange between the computer and external devices.

Instruction Formats

Instructions are structured into fields to represent different operations. These fields, represented in binary, guide the CPU in executing a specific task. Common fields include:

- **Operation Field:** Defines the required action (e.g., addition, subtraction).
- **Address Field:** Indicates where the operand is stored.
- **Mode Field:** Determines how the operand is fetched.

Based on the number of address fields, CPU organizations can be categorized into:

- **Single Accumulator Organization:** Uses an accumulator register for operations.
- **General Register Organization:** Utilizes multiple registers for computational tasks.
- **Stack Organization:** Uses a stack-based approach, eliminating address fields.

Types of Instructions

1. Zero-Address Instructions

Zero-address instructions do not include explicit addresses. Instead, they rely on a stack-based system where operations work on implicit operands at the top of the stack.

Example

Evaluating X = (A + B) * (C + D) using Reverse Polish Notation (RPN):

1. PUSH A
2. PUSH B
3. ADD
4. PUSH C
5. PUSH D
6. ADD

7. MULTIPLY
8. POP X

2. One-Address Instructions

These instructions reference a single operand, often stored in memory or a register. The CPU assumes the **Accumulator (AC)** register holds one operand, minimizing address requirements.

Example

```
LOAD A  // AC = M[A]
ADD B   // AC = AC + M[B]
STORE X // M[X] = AC
```

3. Two-Address Instructions

Two-address instructions involve two operands, enabling operations where data is stored in a different register or memory location than the source operands.

Example

```
MOV R1, A  // R1 = M[A]
ADD R1, B  // R1 = R1 + M[B]
MOV X, R1  // M[X] = R1
```

4. Three-Address Instructions

Three-address instructions specify three operands, allowing direct computation without intermediate storage.

Example

```
ADD R1, A, B // R1 = M[A] + M[B]
ADD R2, C, D // R2 = M[C] + M[D]
MUL X, R1, R2 // M[X] = R1 * R2
```

Instruction codes are crucial in defining how a computer executes tasks. Different instruction formats and addressing modes enable efficient execution, data manipulation, and process control. A complete instruction set must support arithmetic, logic, data transfer, and control operations to optimize performance and functionality.

1.6 Computer Registers

Registers are high-speed memory locations within the CPU that temporarily hold data and instructions being processed. These are often referred to as **processor registers** and are critical for efficient execution.

Functions of Processor Registers

A processor register may store instructions, memory addresses, or data (such as binary values or characters). The CPU relies on registers to manage operations efficiently, ensuring fast access to frequently used data.

Table 3: Commonly Used Registers in a Basic Computer

Register	Symbol	Size (bits)	Function
Data Register	DR	16	Holds operands retrieved from memory.
Address Register	AR	12	Stores the memory address of data.
Accumulator	AC	16	A processing register used for calculations.
Instruction Register	IR	16	Holds the instruction being executed.
Program Counter	PC	12	Stores the address of the next instruction.
Temporary Register	TR	16	Holds temporary data during operations.
Input Register	INPR	8	Stores input data received from external devices.
Output Register	OUTR	8	Holds processed output data before transmission.

Memory and Register Configuration

In a basic computer system, the memory unit typically consists of 4096 words, with each word containing 16 bits. The interaction between memory and registers ensures efficient instruction execution.

- **Data Register (DR):** Stores the operand fetched from memory.
- **Memory Address Register (MAR):** Holds the memory address of the operand.
- **Program Counter (PC):** Tracks the memory address of the next instruction.
- **Accumulator (AC):** Acts as a general-purpose register for arithmetic operations.
- **Instruction Register (IR):** Stores the instruction being processed.
- **Temporary Register (TR):** Temporarily holds intermediate data.
- **Input Register (INPR):** Receives external input data.
- **Output Register (OUTR):** Stores the final output before transferring it to an external device.

Instruction codes and computer registers are integral to the efficient functioning of a CPU. Different instruction formats enable various computational tasks, while registers optimize data storage and manipulation. By incorporating well-structured instruction sets and high-speed registers, modern computers achieve fast and reliable execution of tasks.

1.7 Computer Instructions and Instruction Cycle

The instruction cycle is the sequence of operations the CPU performs to execute a given instruction. It includes multiple phases that ensure smooth processing and execution.

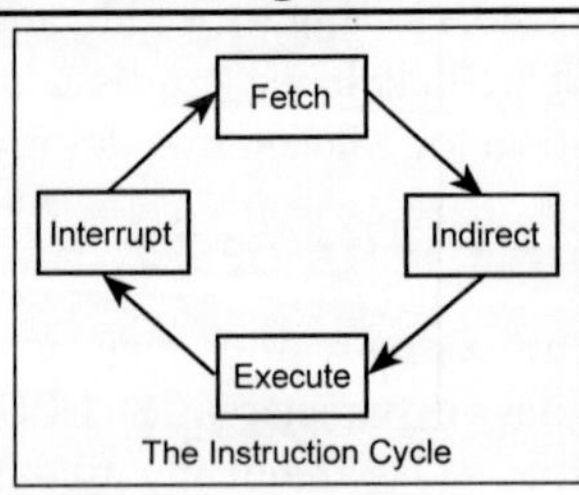

Fig 1.4: Process of instruction cycle

Phases of the Instruction Cycle

1. Fetch Cycle

- The instruction is retrieved from memory, and the Program Counter (PC) is incremented to point to the next instruction.
- The instruction is stored in the Instruction Register (IR).

2. Decode Cycle

- The Control Unit deciphers the fetched instruction to determine the required operation.
- The addressing mode is checked to identify the operand location.

3. Execute Cycle

- The Arithmetic Logic Unit (ALU) performs the necessary computation or data transfer.
- If it's a memory-related instruction, data is either retrieved or stored.
- If it's an I/O instruction, data is exchanged with an external device.

4. Store Cycle

- The execution result is written back to memory or a register.
- The cycle then repeats for the next instruction.

Additional Instruction Cycles

Indirect Cycle

- Used when indirect addressing is employed to fetch operands.
- The address field of the instruction is transferred to the Memory Address Register (MAR) to retrieve the operand's actual location.

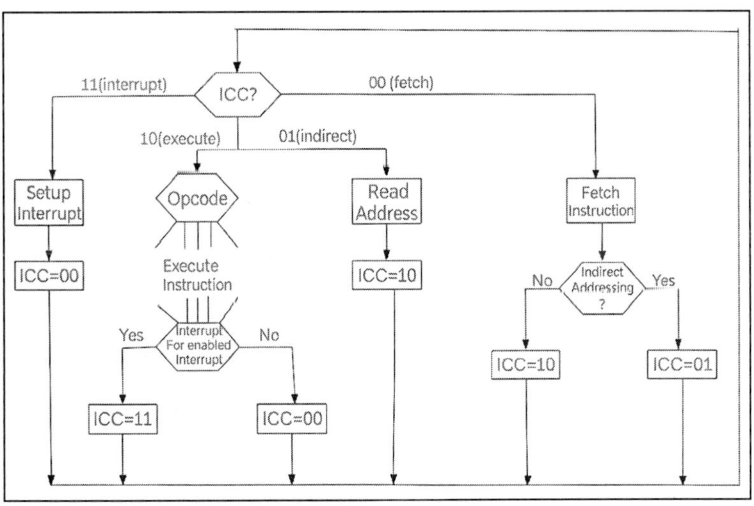

Fig 1.5: *Flowchart of instruction cycle*

Interrupt Cycle

- This occurs when an interrupt signal is detected.
- The current instruction's address is stored, and control is transferred to the interrupt service routine.
- Once the interrupt is handled, normal execution resumes from the stored address.

Example of Instruction Cycle Execution

Consider an instruction ADD R1, R2, which adds the values in registers R1 and R2 and stores the result in R1:

1. **Fetch:** The instruction ADD R1, R2 is retrieved from memory into the instruction register.
2. **Decode:** The control unit interprets ADD as an arithmetic operation involving registers.
3. **Execute:** The ALU adds the contents of R1 and R2.
4. **Store:** The result is written back to R1.

Different Instruction Cycles and Uses

1. **Fetch Cycle:** Retrieves the instruction from memory and loads it into the processor's instruction register.
2. **Decode Cycle:** Interprets the instruction to determine the necessary operation.
3. **Execute Cycle:** Performs the specified operation using the provided operands.
4. **Store Cycle:** Saves the result in memory or a register for future use.

The instruction cycle is integral to CPU operation, ensuring systematic execution of instructions. By understanding each phase—fetch, decode, execute, and store—designers can optimize system performance. The integration of additional cycles, such as indirect and interrupt cycles, further enhances processing capabilities and responsiveness.

Summary

This unit covers general register organization, which includes registers like the accumulator (AC), program counter (PC), instruction register (IR), and data register (DR). These registers store temporary data, addresses, and instructions for efficient processing. Stack organization follows the Last In, First Out (LIFO) principle and is used in function calls, arithmetic operations, and interrupt handling. Operations like push and pop dynamically adjust the stack pointer (SP). Basic computer organization details CPU components, memory hierarchy, and the bus system for communication. Instruction codes and formats define how a processor interprets and executes commands using one, two, or three-address instructions. Finally, computer registers and instruction cycles are explored, showing how data moves through the system for efficient execution, forming the backbone of modern computer processing.

EXERCISES

S.No	16 Marks Questions	Level
1	How would you efficiently allocate registers for the intermediate results in a CPU with a limited number of registers? Provide an example with a simple micro operation.	L3
2	Write the various instruction formats for the following arithmetic expression X = (A / B) + (C / D) + (E / F)	L4
3	Explain how Reverse Polish Notation (RPN) is used in stack-based architectures to perform arithmetic operations. Convert the following infix expression to RPN and show the stack operations for its evaluation. (3 + 4) * (7 * (5 + 3) + 8) (M + N) * (P - Q) / R	L3
4	Draw the flowchart of instruction execution cycle for the following instructions and explain the steps involved in the procedure. SUB R5, R6, R7 AND R1, R2, R3	L2
5	A computer system utilizes a complex instruction set with various addressing modes. Analyze how this affects programming efficiency and execution speed compared to a simpler instruction set architecture. Discuss specific examples to illustrate your points.	L5
6	In a system that uses stack organization, a function is called that pushes several data items onto the stack before performing a series of computations. Analyze how the stack helps in maintaining the state of the function. What happens to the stack when the function completes execution?	L4
7	Analyze a hypothetical instruction set architecture (ISA) that combines both RISC and CISC features. Discuss how this hybrid approach affects programming efficiency, execution speed, and hardware complexity.	L5
8	Evaluate the effectiveness of using fixed-length versus variable-length instruction codes in a processor architecture. Discuss the advantages and disadvantages of each approach in terms of memory usage, decoding complexity, and execution speed.	L4

S.No.	2 Marks Questions	Level
1	For an instruction format with 8 bits where the first 4 bits are the opcode and the remaining 4 bits are the address, what is the address portion of the instruction 11001010?	L2
2	For the following set of instructions, identify which instruction code format it belongs to: 101100110101001 011101010011010 111101000101011	L2
3	What are the key phases of the instruction cycle, and how do they contribute to the execution of a program?	L1

<table>
<tr><th>S.No.</th><th>2 Marks Questions</th><th>Level</th></tr>
<tr><td>4</td><td>Given the data of value in PC is 0000001011100011. After executing the fetch cycle, fill the updated data in the below given table.
<table>
<tr><td>MAR</td><td></td></tr>
<tr><td>MBR</td><td></td></tr>
<tr><td>PC</td><td>0000000010010001</td></tr>
<tr><td>IR</td><td></td></tr>
<tr><td>AC</td><td></td></tr>
</table></td><td>L2</td></tr>
<tr><td>5</td><td>Write the control word for the following micro operations:
a. R7 -> R5 + R6
b. R3 -> R2 – R1
c. R1 -> R2 V R3
d. R6 -> SHL R6</td><td>L2</td></tr>
<tr><td>6</td><td>You are given a simple computer system with a basic architecture involving an ALU, registers, and memory. Explain how the ALU interacts with the registers and memory to perform arithmetic operations.</td><td>L3</td></tr>
<tr><td>7</td><td>Compare a register stack with a memory stack in terms of speed and storage capacity. Briefly describe one advantage of using a register stack over a memory stack and one limitation of a register stack.</td><td>L4</td></tr>
<tr><td>8</td><td>In a CPU with a register stack, if the stack pointer initially points to register R5 and a PUSH operation is performed, which register will hold the value of the stack pointer after the push? Describe the effect of this operation on the stack pointer and the top of the stack with diagrammatic representation.</td><td>L2</td></tr>
<tr><td>9</td><td>If an arithmetic operation adds the value in the accumulator to another register, describe the role of the accumulator in this operation.</td><td>L3</td></tr>
<tr><td>10</td><td>How might the choice between using a general register or an accumulator impact the performance of an application?</td><td>L2</td></tr>
<tr><td>11</td><td>How could the absence of standardized instruction codes affect the development of software and hardware compatibility?</td><td>L2</td></tr>
<tr><td>12</td><td>In what scenarios might one organization be preferred over the other for efficient data handling?</td><td>L1</td></tr>
<tr><td>13</td><td>How do changes in the instruction register and program counter influence the flow of execution in a program?</td><td>L2</td></tr>
<tr><td>14</td><td>How does the encoding of instructions like addition affect the complexity of a CPU's architecture?</td><td>L2</td></tr>
<tr><td>15</td><td>How might errors in stack management affect program execution and data integrity?</td><td>L2</td></tr>
<tr><td>16</td><td>Describe how pipelining can affect data movement between registers in a CPU.</td><td>L3</td></tr>
</table>

Arithmetic Logic Unit and Computer Arithmetic

2

UNIT

RATIONALE

The study of the **Arithmetic Logic Unit (ALU) and Computer Arithmetic** is essential for understanding how computers process and manipulate numerical data. The ALU is a fundamental component of the CPU, performing arithmetic, logical, and shift operations necessary for executing instructions efficiently. Computer arithmetic covers various number representations, including fixed-point and floating-point systems, and explores techniques for addition, subtraction, multiplication, and division. Understanding ALU design enhances knowledge of digital circuits, while exploring architectures like MIPS highlights practical implementations in processors. These concepts are crucial for optimizing computation speed, designing efficient hardware, and improving overall system performance.

OUTCOMES

This unit focuses on the design and operations of the Arithmetic Logic Unit (ALU) and its role in processing arithmetic and logic operations. It also introduces various architectures, such as MIPS, RISC, and CISC, and discusses arithmetic operations and control unit design. By completing this unit, students will:

- Understand the architecture and functionality of the ALU.
- Analyze different arithmetic and logic operations used in computational tasks.
- Compare the characteristics and differences between MIPS, RISC, and CISC architectures.
- Examine shift micro-operations and their role in data manipulation.
- Learn about floating-point arithmetic operations and their significance in computing.
- Explore microprogrammed control design and its impact on instruction execution.

2.1 Introduction to ALU

Data is manipulated by using the arithmetic instructions in digital computers. Data is manipulated to produce results necessary to give solution for the computation problems. The Addition, subtraction, multiplication and division are the four basic arithmetic operations. If we want then we can derive other operations by using these four operations. To execute arithmetic operations there is a separate section called arithmetic processing unit in central processing unit.

The arithmetic instructions are performed generally on binary or decimal data. Fixed-point numbers are used to represent integers or fractions.

2.2 Arithmetic, Logic and Shift Micro Operations

Micro-operations are basic operations performed on data stored in registers. These operations are executed at the microarchitecture level of a computer and help in manipulating data efficiently. The three fundamental types of micro-operations are arithmetic micro-operations, logic micro-operations, and shift micro-operations.

Arithmetic Micro-Operations

Arithmetic micro-operations perform basic mathematical computations on binary data stored in registers. The primary arithmetic micro-operations include:

- **Addition:** Adds the contents of two registers and stores the result in a destination register.

  R3←R1+R2R3 \leftarrow R1 + R2R3←R1+R2

- **Subtraction:** Performed by taking the complement of one operand and adding it to the other, effectively implementing two's complement subtraction.

  R3←R1−R2=R1+(R2¯+1)R3 \leftarrow R1 - R2 = R1 + (\overline{R2} + 1)R3←R1−R2=R1+(R2+1)

- **Increment:** Adds 1 to the contents of a register.

  R1←R1+1R1 \leftarrow R1 + 1R1←R1+1

- **Decrement:** Subtracts 1 from the contents of a register.

  R1←R1−1R1 \leftarrow R1 - 1R1←R1−1

- **Multiplication:** Usually implemented using iterative addition and shift operations.

  R3←R1×R2R3 \leftarrow R1 \times R2R3←R1×R2

- **Division:** Performed using repeated subtraction or hardware division circuits.

  R3←R1÷R2R3 \leftarrow R1 \div R2R3←R1÷R2

These operations are crucial for performing computations in arithmetic logic units (ALUs) within processors.

Logic Micro-Operations

Logic micro-operations perform bitwise operations on binary data stored in registers. They are useful in manipulating individual bits within a word. The common logic micro-operations include:

- **Bitwise AND:**

  R3←R1∧R2R3 \leftarrow R1 \land R2R3←R1∧R2

  This operation results in a bit being 1 only if both corresponding bits in R1 and R2 are 1.

- **Bitwise OR:**

  R3←R1∨R2R3 \leftarrow R1 \lor R2R3←R1∨R2

  A bit is set to 1 if either of the corresponding bits in R1 or R2 is 1.

- **Bitwise XOR (Exclusive OR):**

  R3←R1⊕R2R3 \leftarrow R1 \oplus R2R3←R1⊕R2

  The result is 1 only if the bits in R1 and R2 differ.

- **Bitwise NOT (Complement):**

  R3←$\overline{\text{R1}}$R3 \leftarrow \overline{R1}R3←R1

  This operation inverts each bit in R1.

- **Selective Set, Clear, and Toggle:**
  - **Set:** Forces specific bits to 1.
  - **Clear:** Forces specific bits to 0.
  - **Toggle:** Inverts selected bits using XOR with a mask.

Logic micro-operations are widely used in digital systems for operations such as masking, data manipulation, and control logic implementation.

Shift Micro-Operations

Shift micro-operations are used to move the bits of a register left or right. These operations are useful for data alignment, multiplication, division, and bitwise transformations. The types of shift operations include:

1. **Logical Shift:** Moves bits left or right, filling the vacant positions with 0s.
   - **Logical left shift (LSL):**

     R1←R1<<1R1 \leftarrow R1 << 1R1←R1<<1
   - **Logical right shift (LSR):**

     R1←R1>>1R1 \leftarrow R1 >> 1R1←R1>>1
2. **Arithmetic Shift:** Similar to logical shift but preserves the sign bit (most significant bit) during right shifts.
   - **Arithmetic left shift:**

     R1←R1<<1R1 \leftarrow R1 << 1R1←R1<<1

     Used for multiplication by 2.
   - **Arithmatic right shift:**

     R1←R1>>1R1 \leftarrow R1 >> 1R1←R1>>1

     Used for division by 2, preserving the sign.
3. **Circular Shift (Rotate):** Bits are shifted, and the vacated bit positions are filled by the bits shifted out.
   - **Rotate left (ROL):**

     R1←(R1<<1)+MSBR1 \leftarrow (R1 << 1) + \text{MSB}R1←(R1<<1)+MSB
   - **Rotate right (ROR):**

     R1←(R1>>1)+LSBR1 \leftarrow (R1 >> 1) + \text{LSB}R1←(R1>>1)+LSB
4. **Rotate with Carry:** Includes the carry bit in the rotation, useful in extended precision arithmetic.
   - Rotate left through carry (RLC)
   - Rotate right through carry (RRC)

Shift operations are essential for bit manipulation, encryption, and efficient arithmetic calculations.

2.3 Arithmetic Logic Shift Unit

The Arithmetic Logic Shift Unit (ALSU) is a fundamental component of a computer's processor responsible for performing arithmetic, logical, and shift operations. It is an extension of the Arithmetic Logic Unit (ALU), integrating shift operations to handle bit manipulation efficiently.

This unit plays a critical role in executing mathematical computations, logical evaluations, and data transformations within digital systems.

Structure of the Arithmetic Logic Shift Unit

The ALSU consists of three main functional blocks:

- **Arithmetic Unit:** Performs operations like addition, subtraction, multiplication, and division.
- **Logic Unit:** Handles bitwise operations, including AND, OR, XOR, and NOT.
- **Shift Unit:** Executes shift and rotate operations for data alignment and transformation.

The integration of these operations into a single unit allows processors to execute complex instructions efficiently, reducing the need for multiple separate components.

2.4 Example Architectures: MIPS

MIPS (Microprocessor without Interlocked Pipeline Stages) is a Reduced Instruction Set Computing (RISC) architecture designed for high-performance computing. Developed by MIPS Computer Systems in the 1980s, it is widely used in embedded systems, gaming consoles, and networking devices due to its simplicity, efficiency, and scalability. The MIPS architecture follows a load-store design, meaning arithmetic and logical operations are performed only on registers, while memory access is limited to load and store instructions.

Characteristics of MIPS Architecture

The MIPS architecture is based on RISC principles, which emphasize simplicity and efficiency.

Some defining characteristics include:

- **Fixed-Length Instructions:** All instructions are 32 bits long, making decoding simpler and improving pipeline efficiency.
- **Load-Store Architecture:** The CPU interacts with memory only through load (LW) and store (SW) instructions, ensuring a streamlined instruction set.
- **Register-Based Operations:** MIPS has 32 general-purpose registers (GPRs), denoted as $0 to $31, where $0 is always set to zero.
- **Three-Operand Format:** Arithmetic and logical instructions use three register operands, allowing for flexible computations without additional memory access.
- **Pipelining:** MIPS supports five-stage pipelining (Fetch, Decode, Execute, Memory Access, Write-back), increasing instruction throughput.
- **Delayed Branching:** To improve pipeline efficiency, MIPS uses a branch delay slot, executing the instruction immediately following a branch before changing the program counter.

MIPS Instruction Set Architecture (ISA)

MIPS instructions are categorized into three main types:

A. R-Type (Register-Register Instructions)

These instructions perform operations on registers and store the result in a register. They use the format:

opcode (6 bits)|rs (5 bits)|rt (5 bits)|rd (5 bits)|shamt (5 bits)|funct (6 bits\)

B. I-Type (Immediate and Memory Instructions)

These instructions involve immediate values or memory access. The format is:

opcode (6 bits)|rs (5 bits)|rt (5 bits)|immediate (16 bits)

C. J-Type (Jump Instructions)

These instructions change the program execution flow using a 26-bit address field. The format is:

opcode (6 bits)|address (bits)

MIPS Pipelining

MIPS uses a five-stage pipeline to enhance instruction throughput:

1. **Instruction Fetch (IF):** The instruction is retrieved from memory.
2. **Instruction Decode (ID):** The instruction is decoded, and registers are read.
3. **Execute (EX):** The ALU performs arithmetic or logical operations.
4. **Memory Access (MEM):** Load and store operations access memory.
5. **Write-Back (WB):** The result is written back to a register.

This overlapping execution improves performance, as multiple instructions are processed simultaneously.

Memory Organization in MIPS

MIPS follows a byte-addressable memory model, with memory segmented into:

- **Text Segment:** Stores program instructions.
- **Data Segment:** Holds global and static variables.
- **Stack Segment:** Manages function calls and local variables.
- **Heap Segment:** Dynamically allocated memory at runtime.

Registers such as $sp (stack pointer) and $gp (global pointer) help manage memory operations efficiently.

Applications of MIPS Architecture

Due to its simplicity and efficiency, MIPS is used in various domains, including:

- **Embedded Systems:** Found in routers, set-top boxes, and automotive systems.
- **Gaming Consoles:** Used in early PlayStation consoles.
- **Network Processors:** Deployed in high-speed packet processing units.

- **Computer Science Education:** Frequently used in academic courses for learning assembly language.

RISC Architecture

RISC (Reduced Instruction Set Computer) is used in portable devices due to its power efficiency. For Example, Apple iPod and Nintendo DS. RISC is a type of microprocessor architecture that uses highly-optimized set of instructions.

RISC does the opposite, reducing the cycles per instruction at the cost of the number of instructions per program Pipelining is one of the unique feature of RISC. It is performed by overlapping the execution of several instructions in a pipeline fashion. It has a high performance advantage over CISC.

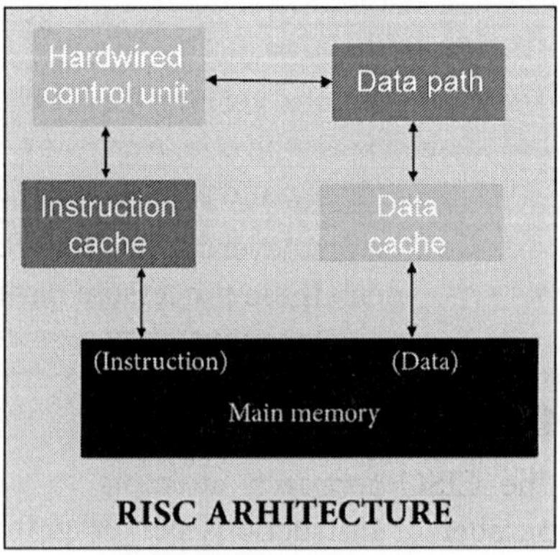

Fig 2.1: RISC Architecture

RISC Architecture Characteristics

Simple Instructions are used in RISC architecture. RISC helps and supports few simple data types and synthesize complex data types. RISC utilizes simple addressing modes and fixed length instructions for pipelining. RISC permits any register to use in any context.

One Cycle Execution Time

The amount of work that a computer can perform is reduced by separating "LOAD" and "STORE" instructions. RISC contains Large Number of Registers in order to prevent various number of interactions with memory. In RISC, Pipelining is easy as the execution of all instructions will be done in a uniform interval of time i.e. one click. The features of RISC include the following:

- The demand of decoding is less
- Uniform instruction set
- Few data types in hardware
- General purpose register Identical
- Simple addressing nodes

Advantages of RISC Architecture

- RISC (Reduced instruction set computing) architecture has a set of instructions, so high- levellanguage compilers can produce more efficient code
- It allows freedom of using the space on microprocessors because of its simplicity.
- Many RISC processors use the registers for passing arguments and holding the local variables.
- RISCfunctionsuseonlyafewparameters,andtheRISCprocessorscannotusethecall instructions, and therefore, use a fixed length instruction which is easy to pipeline.
- The speed of the operation can be maximized and the execution time can be minimized. Very less number of instructional formats, a few numbers of instructions and a few addressing modes are needed.

Disadvantages of RISC Architecture

- Mostly, the performance of the RISC processors depends on the programmer or compiler as the knowledge of the compiler plays a vital role while changing the CISC code to a RISC code.
- While rearranging the CISC code to a RISC code, termed as a code expansion, will increase the size. And, the quality of this code expansion will again depend on the compiler, and also on the machine's instruction set.
- The first level cache of the RISC processors is also a disadvantage of the RISC, in which these processors have large memory caches on the chip itself. For feeding the instructions, they require very fast memory systems.

CISC Architecture

The CISC approach attempts to minimize the number of instructions per program, sacrificing the number of cycles per instruction. Computers based on the CISC architecture are designed to decrease the memory cost. Because, the large programs need more storage, thus increasing the memory cost and large memory becomes more expensive. To solve these problems, the number of instructions per program can be reduced by embedding the number of operations in a single instruction, thereby making the instructions more complex.

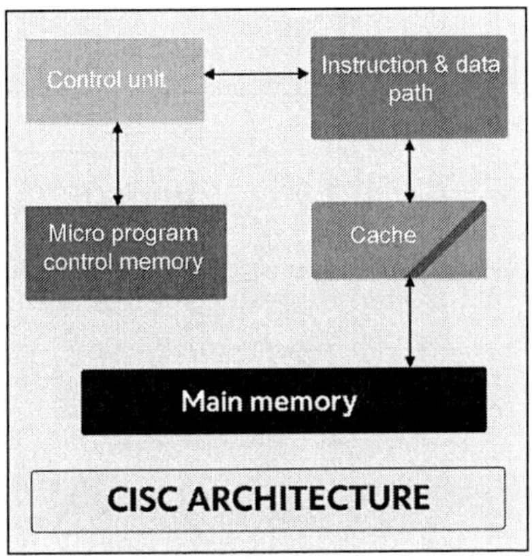

Fig 2.2: *CISC Architecture*

MUL loads two values from the memory into separate registers in CISC. CISC uses minimum possible instructions by implementing hardware and executes operations. Instruction Set Architecture is a medium to permit communication between the programmer and the hardware. Data execution part, copying of data, deleting or editing is the user commands used in the microprocessor and with this microprocessor the Instruction set architecture is operated.

The main keywords used in the above Instruction Set Architecture are as below.

(i) **Instruction Set:** Group of instructions given to execute the program and they direct the computer by manipulating the data. Instructions are in the form Opcode (operational code) and Operand. Where, opcode is the instruction applied to load and store data, etc. The operand is a memory register where instruction applied.

(ii) **Addressing Modes:** Addressing modes are the manner in the data is accessed. Depending upon the type of instruction applied, addressing modes are of various types such as direct mode where straight data is accessed or indirect mode where the location of the data is accessed. Processors having identical ISA may be very different in organization. Processors with identical ISA and nearly identical organization is still not nearly identical.

Thus, CPU performance is dependent upon Instruction Count, CPI (Cycles per instruction) and Clock cycle time. And all three are affected by the instruction set architecture.

Characteristics of CISC Architecture

Instruction-decoding logic will be Complex. One instruction is required to support multiple addressing modes. Less chip space is enough for general purpose registers for the instructions that are Ooperated directly on memory. Various CISC designs are set up two special registers for the stack pointer, handling interrupts, etc. MUL is referred to as a "complex instruction" and requires the programmer for storing functions. CISC designs involve very complex architectures, including a large number of instructions and addressing modes, whereas RISC designs involve simplified instruction set and adapt it to the real requirements of user programs.

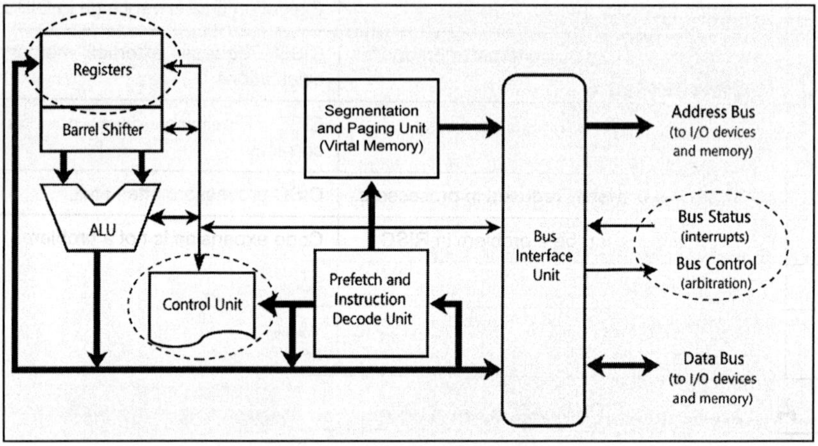

Fig 2.3: *CISC and RISC Design*

Advantages of CISC Architecture

- Microprogramming is easy assembly language to implement, and less expensive than hard wiring a control unit.
- The ease of micro coding new instructions allowed designers to make CISC machines upwardly compatible:
- As each instruction became more accomplished, fewer instructions could be used to implement a given task.

Disadvantages of CISC Architecture

- The performance of the machine slows down due to the amount of clock time taken by different instructions will be dissimilar
- Only 20% of the existing instructions is used in a typical programming event, even though there are various specialized instructions in reality which are not even used frequently.

RISC vs. CISC Architecture Comparison

S.No.	RISC	CISC
1.	RISC has no memory unit and uses a separate hardware to implement instructions.	CISC has a memory unit to implement complex instructions

S.No.	RISC	CISC
2.	RISC has a hard-wired unit of programming.	CISC has a microprogramming unit.
3.	RISC is a complex compiler design.	CISC is an easy compiler design Calculations.
4.	RISC calculations are faster and more precise.	CISC calculations are slow and precise.
5.	RISC decoding of instructions is simple.	CISC decoding of instructions is complex Time.
6.	Execution time is very less in RISC.	Execution time is very high in CISC.
7.	RISC does not require external memory for calculations.	CISC requires external memory for calculations.
8.	RISC Pipelining does function correctly.	CISC Pipelining does not function correctly.
9.	RISC stalling is mostly reduced in processors.	CISC processors often stall.
10.	Code expansion can be a problem in RISC	Code expansion is not a problem.
11.	Space is saved	Space is wasted
12.	ARM Architecture, MIPS, RISC-V, Power Architecture	VAX, PDP-11, Motorola 68k, and your desktop PCs on Intel's x86.

2.5 Addition and Subtraction

There are three ways of representing negative fixed-point binary numbers: Signed-magnitude, signed-l's complement, or signed-2's complement. Most computers use the signed-2's complement representation when performing arithmetic operations with integers. For floating-point operations, most computers use the signed-magnitude representation for the mantissa.

Addition and Subtraction with Signed-Magnitude Data

Where the signed numbers are added or subtracted, we find that there are eight different conditions to consider, depending on the sign of the numbers and the operation performed. These conditions are listed in the first column of Table 2.1. The other columns in the table show the actual operation to be performed with the magnitude of the numbers. The last column is needed to present a negative zero. In other words, when two equal numbers are subtracted, the result should be +0 not -0. The algorithms for addition and subtraction are derived from the table and can be stated as follows :

Table 2.1: *Addition and Subtraction of Signed-Magnitude Numbers*

Operation	Add Magnitudes	Subtract Magnitudes		
		When A > B	When A < B	When A = B
(+ A) + (+ B)	+(A + B)			
(+ A) + (– B)		+ (A – B)	– (B – A)	+ (A – B)
(– A) + (+ B)		– (A – B)	+ (B – A)	+ (A – B)
(– A) + (– B)	– (A + B)			

Operation	Add Magnitudes	Subtract Magnitudes		
(+ A) – (+ B)		+ (A – B)	– (B – A)	+ (A – B)
(+ A) – (– B)	+(A + B)			
(– A) – (+ B)	– (A + B)			
(– A) – (– B)		– (A – B)	+ (B – A)	+ (A – B)

When the signs of A and B are same, add the two magnitudes and attach the sign of result is that of A. When the signs of A and B are not same, compare the magnitudes and subtract the smaller number from the larger. Choose the sign of the result to be the same as A, if A > B or the complement of the sign of A if A < B. If the two magnitudes are equal, subtract B from A and make the sign of the result will be positive.

Hardware Implementation

First, a parallel-adder is needed to perform the micro operation A + B . Second, a comparator circuit is needed to establish if A > B, A = B, or A < B. Third, two parallel- subtractor circuits are needed to perform the micro operations A - B and B - A. The sign relationship can be determined from an exclusive OR gate with A, and B, as inputs.

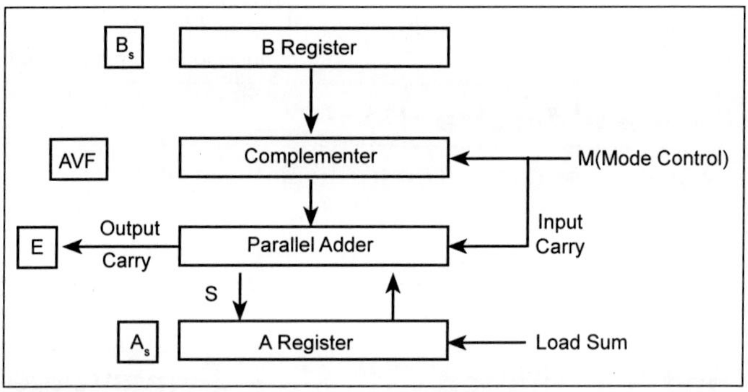

Fig 2.4: *Hardware for signed magnitude addition and subtraction*

Implementing the addition and subtraction operations. It consists of registers A and B and sign flip-flops A, and B, . Subtraction is done by adding A to the 2' s complement of B. The output carry is transferred to flip-flop E, where it can be checked to determine the relative magnitudes of the two numbers. The add-overflow flip-flop AVF holds the overflow bit when A and B are added. The A register provides other microoperations that may be needed when we specify the sequence of steps in the algorithm.

Description

A_S Sign of A , B_S Sign of B ,A_S & A Accumulator , AVF Overflow bit for A + B E Output carry for parallel adder

- **Data representation Signed magnitude:** consists of the magnitude and negative sign (sign bit in binary, '0' for positive and '1' for negative)

  – E.g. +14 = 0 0001110, -14= 1 0001110
- **Signed 2's complement:** Add 1 to signed 1's complement representation of the data – E.g. -14 = 1 1110010

Hardware Algorithm

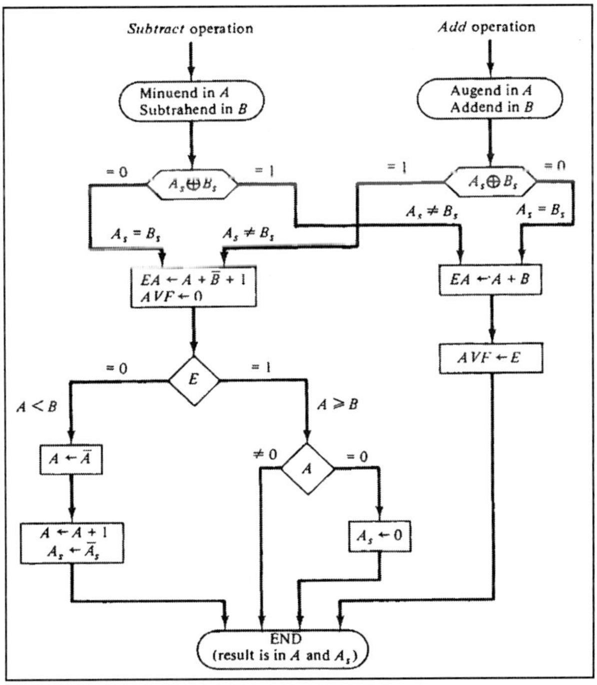

Fig 2.5: *Flowchart for add and subtract operations*

Signed Magnitude Addition and Subtraction

	B = 11011 Q = 00111
4	Q4 = 1, A = 0, Qs = 1 EA = A + B = 1011 EAQ = 0 1011 0111 Shr EAQ = 0 0101 1011
3	Q3 = EA = 1 0000 EAQ 1 0000 1011 Shr EAQ 0 1000 0101
2	Q2 = 1 EA = 1 0011 EAQ 1 0011 01 01 Shr EAQ 0 1001 101 0
1	Q1 = 0 Shr EAQ 0 0100 1101 = 77
0	

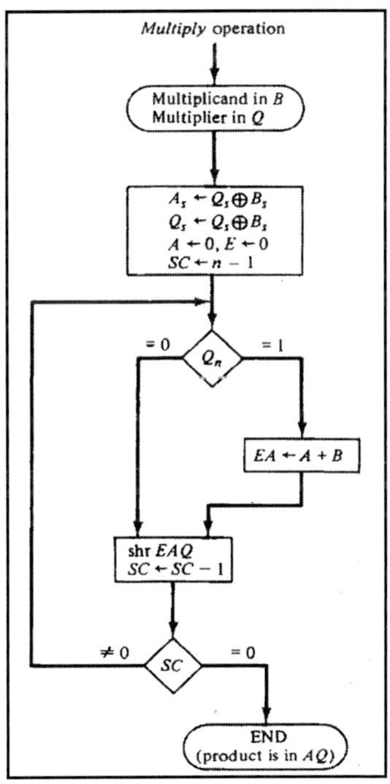

Fig 2.6: *Flow chart for multiply operation*

- For an add operation, identical signs dictate that the magnitudes be added, different signs require that the magnitudes be subtracted
- For subtraction operation, different signs dictate that magnitudes be added, identical signs require that magnitudes be subtracted

AVF – Add-overflow flip-flop holds the overflow bit when A and B are added Addition of A and B is done through parallel adder.

Table 2.2: *Numerical example for binary multiplier*

Multiplicand B = 10111	E	A	Q	SC
Multiplier in Q	0	00000	10011	101
$Q_n = 1$; add B		10111		
First partial product	0	10111		
Shift right EAQ	0	01011	11001	100
$Q_n = 1$; add B		10111		
Second partial product	1	00010		
Shift right EAQ	0	10001	01100	011
$Q_n = 0$; shift right EAQ	0	01000	10110	010
$Q_n = 0$; shift right EAQ	0	00100	01011	001
$Q_n = 1$; add B		10111		
Fifth partial product	0	11011		
Shift right EAQ	0	01101	10101	000
Final product in AQ = 0110110101				

2.6 Booth Multiplication

A= 00011 B= 00111 => A*B= A*(7) =A* (8-1) =A*8-A*1

Booth algorithm requires examination of the multiplier bits and shifting of the partial product

Q_n – LSB of multiplier Extra flip flop

Q_{n+1} is appended to the multiplier bits to facilitate double bit inspection of the multiplier.

In 2's complement representation, we can use Booth algorithm without change

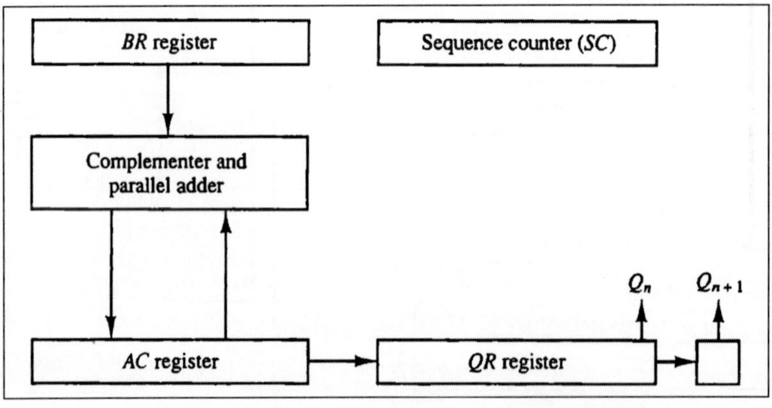

Fig 2.7: *Block diagram of hardware for Booth algorithm*

Compare bits of Q_n and Q_{n+1} Rules are:

1. The multiplicand is subtracted from the partial product upon encountering the first least significant 1 in a string of 1's in the multiplier
2. The multiplicand is added to the partial product upon encountering the first 0(provided that there was a previous 1) in a string of 0's in the multiplier
3. The partial product does not change when the multiplier bit is identical to the previous multiplier bit

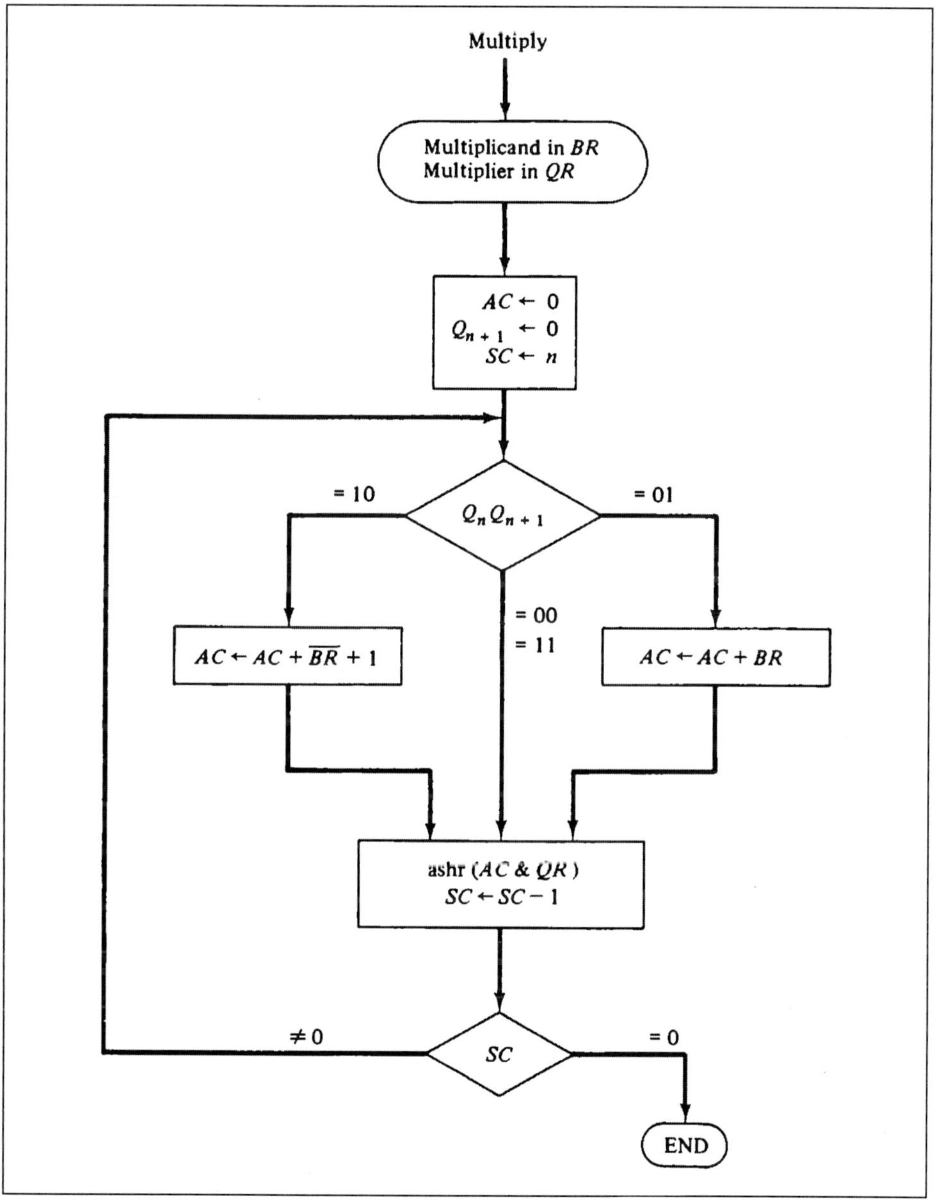

Fig 2.8: *Booth algorithm for multiplication of signed 2's complements numbers*

Table 2.3: Example of multiplication with Booth Algorithm

$Q_n\ Q_{n+1}$	$BR = 10111$ $\overline{BR} + 1 = 01001$	AC	QR	Q_{n+1}	SC
	Initial	00000	10011	0	101
1 0	Subtract BR	01001			
		01001			
	ashr	00100	11001	1	100
1 1	ashr	00010	01100	1	011
0 1	Add BR	10111			
		11001			
	ashr	11100	10110	0	010
0 0	ashr	11110	01011	0	001
1 0	Subtract BR	01001			
		00111			
	ashr	00011	10101	1	000

Array Multiplier: Fast Approach

To check the bits of the multiplier one at a time and forming partial products is a sequential operation requiring a sequence of add and shift micro-operations. The multiplication of two binary numbers can be done with one micro-operation by using combinational circuit that forms the product bits all at once. This is a fast way since all it takes is the time for the signals to propagate through the gates that form the multiplication array. However, an array multiplier requires a large number of gates, and so it is not an economical unit for the development of ICs

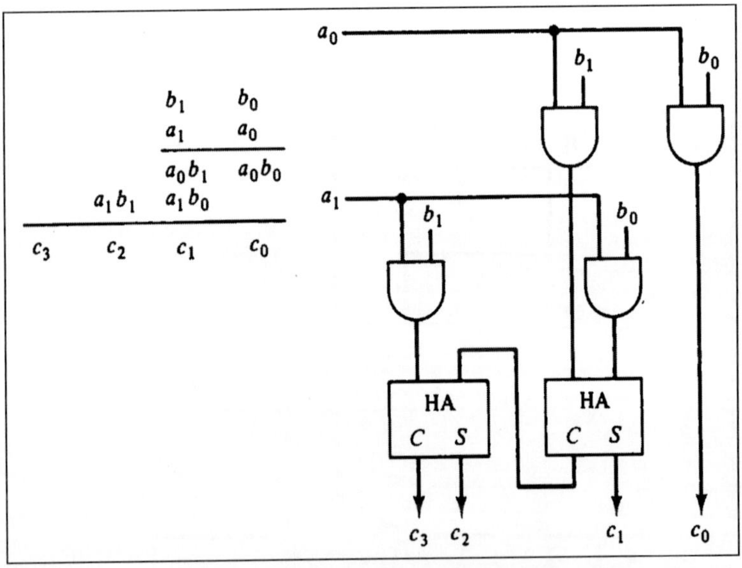

Fig 2.9: 2 bit by 2 bit array multiplier

2.7 Division

Binary division – simpler because the quotient digits are either 0 or 1 and there is no need to estimate how many times the dividend or partial remainder fits into the divisor.

- Division operation may result in a quotient with an overflow. Divide overflow flip flop (DVF) is used to detect overflow Divisor – B register, Dividend – A and Q register
- If the signs of divisor and dividend are alike, the sign of the quotient is plus. Otherwise it is minus.

Table 2.4: *Binary division*

Divisor:	11010	Quotient = Q
B = 10001	)0111000000	Dividend = A
	01110	5 bits of $A < B$, quotient has 5 bits
	011100	6 bits of $A \geqslant B$
	-10001	Shift right B and subtract; enter 1 in Q
	-010110	7 bits of remainder $\geqslant B$
	--10001	Shift right B and subtract; enter 1 in Q
	--001010	Remainder $< B$; enter 0 in Q; shift right B
	---010100	Remainder $\geqslant B$
	----10001	Shift right B and subtract; enter 1 in Q
	----000110	Remainder $< B$; enter 0 in Q
	-----00110	Final remainder

Divisor B = 10001, $\overline{B} + 1$ = 01111

	E	A	Q	SC
Dividend:		01110	00000	5
shl EAQ	0	11100	00000	
add $\overline{B}+1$		01111		
E = 1	1	01011		
Set Q_n = 1	1	01011	00001	4
shl EAQ	0	10110	00010	
Add $\overline{B}+1$		01111		
E = 1	1	00101		
Set Q_n = 1	1	00101	00011	3
shl EAQ	0	01010	00110	
Add $\overline{B}+1$		01111		
E = 0; leave Q_n = 0	0	11001	00110	
Add B		10001		
				2
Restore remainder	1	01010		
shl EAQ	0	10100	01100	
Add $\overline{B}+1$		01111		
E = 1	1	00011		
Set Q_n = 1	1	00011	01101	1
shl EAQ	0	00110	11010	
Add $\overline{B}+1$		01111		
E = 0; leave Q_n = 0	0	10101	11010	
Add B		10001		
Restore remainder	1	00110	11010	0
Neglect E				
Remainder in A:		00110		
Quotient in Q:			11010	

Fig 2.10: *Example of binary division with digital hardware*

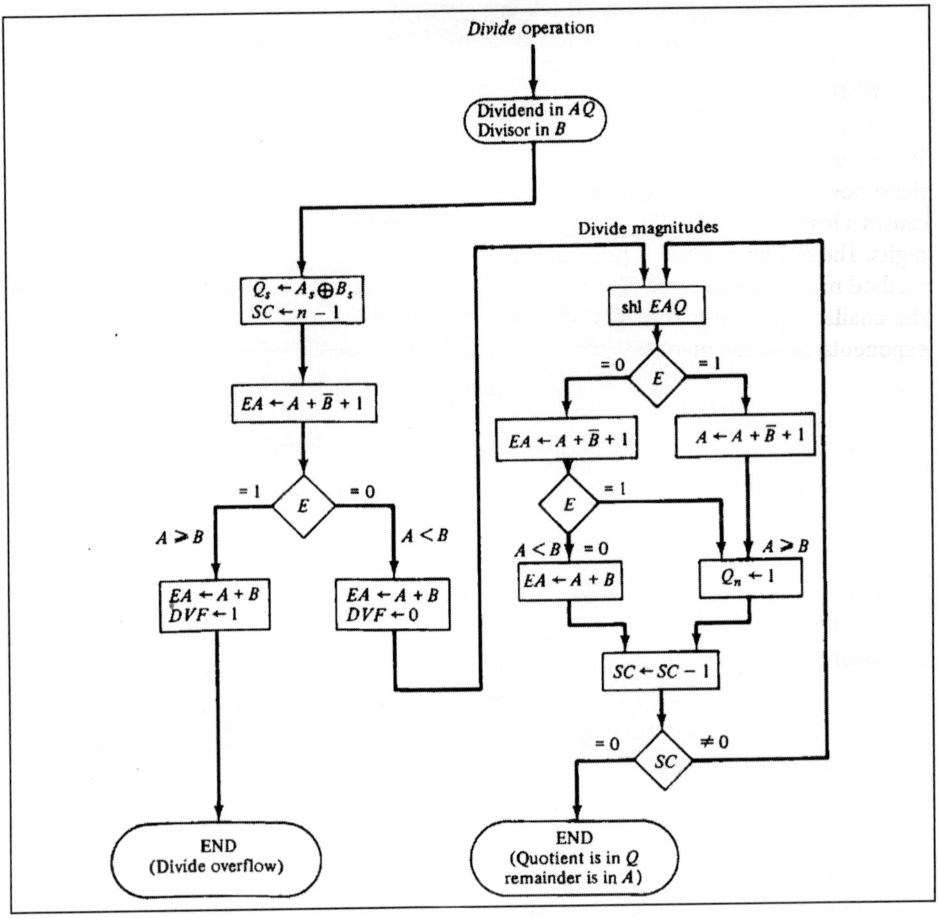

Fig 2.11: *Flow chart for divide operation*

2.8 Floating Point Arithmetic Operations

Numbers too large for standard integer representations or that have fractional components are usually represented in scientific notation, a form used commonly by scientists and engineers.

Examples:

4.25×10^1

- Addition and subtraction are more complex than multiplication and division
- Need to align mantissas

Algorithm

- Check for zeros
- Align significant (adjusting exponents)
- Add or subtract significant
- Normalize result

$$F = m \times r^e$$

where, m: Mantissa, r: Radix, e: Exponent

It is necessary to make two exponents be equal before the mantissas can be added. We can either shift the first number three positions to the left, or shift the second number three positions to the right. When we store the mantissas in registers, shifting to the left causes a loss of most significant digits. Shifting to the right causes a loss of least significant digits. The second method is preferable because it only reduces the accuracy, while the first method may cause an error. The usual alignment procedure is to shift the mantissa that has the smaller exponent to the right by a number of places equal to the difference between the exponents. Now, the mantissas can be added.

$$\begin{array}{r} .5372400 \times 10^2 \\ +\,.0001580 \times 10^2 \\ \hline .5373980 \times 10^2 \\ \hline \end{array}$$

When two normalized mantissas are added, the sum may contain an overflow digit. An overflow can be corrected easily by shifting the sum once to the right and incrementing the exponent. When two numbers are subtracted, the result may contain most significant zeros as shown in the following example:

$$\begin{array}{r} .56780 \times 10^5 \\ -\,.56430 \times 10^5 \\ \hline .00350 \times 10^5 \\ \hline \end{array}$$

An underflow occurs if a floating-point number that has a 0 in the most significant position of the mantissa. To normalize a number that contains an underflow, we shift the mantissa to the left and decrement the exponent until a nonzero digit appears in the first position. Here, it is necessary to shift left twice to obtain $.35000 \times 10^3$. In most computers a normalization procedure is performed after each operation to ensure that all results are in a normalized form.

Floating-point multiplication and division need not do an alignment of the mantissas. Multiplying the two mantissas and adding the exponents can form the product. Dividing the mantissas and subtracting the exponents perform division.

Register Configuration

Three registers are there, BR, AC, and QR. Each register is subdivided into two parts. The mantissa part has the same uppercase letter symbols as in fixed-point representation. The exponent part may use corresponding lower-case letter symbol.

Assuming that each floating-point number has a mantissa in signed-magnitude representation and a biased exponent. Thus the AC has a mantissa whose sign is in A_s, and a magnitude that is in A. The diagram shows the most significant bit of A, labeled by A1. The bit in his position must be a 1 to normalize the number. Note that the symbol AC represents the entire register, that is, the concatenation of A_s, A and a. In the similar way, register BR is subdivided into B_s, B, and b and QR into Q_s, Q and q. A parallel-adder adds the two mantissas and loads the sum into A and the carry into E.

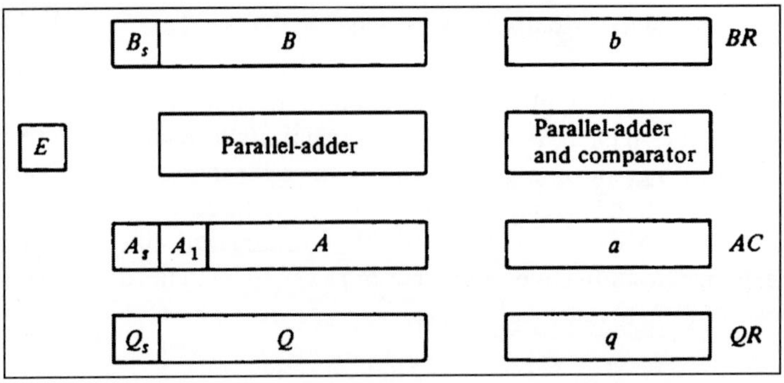

Fig 2.12: Registers for floating point arithmetic operations

Addition and Subtraction of Floating Point Numbers

During addition or subtraction, the two floating-point operands are kept in AC and BR. The sum or difference is formed in the AC.

The algorithm can be divided into four consecutive parts:

1. Check for zeros.
2. Add or subtract the mantissas
3. Normalize the result
4. Align the mantissas.

A floating-point number cannot be normalized, if it is 0. If this number is used for computation, the result may also be zero. Instead of checking for zeros during the normalization process we check for zeros at the beginning and terminate the process if necessary. The alignment of the mantissas must be carried out prior to their operation. After the mantissas are added or subtracted, the result may be un-normalized. The normalization procedure ensures that the result is normalized before it is transferred to memory.

For adding or subtracting two floating-point binary numbers, if BR is equal to zero, the operation is stopped, with the value in the AC being the result. If AC = 0, we transfer the content of BR into AC and also complement its sign we have to subtract the numbers. If neither number is equal it to zero, we proceed to align the mantissas. The magnitude comparator attached to exponents a and b gives three outputs, which show their relative magnitudes. If the two exponents are equal, we go to perform the arithmetic operation. If the exponents are not equal, the mantissa having the smaller exponent is shifted to the right and its exponent incremented. This process is repeated until two exponents are equal.

The addition and subtraction of the two mantissas is similar to the fixed-point addition and subtraction algorithm presented in the following Fig

Multiplication

The algorithm can be divided into four consecutive parts:

1. Check for zeros.
2. Add the exponents.

3. Multiply the mantissas
4. Normalize the result

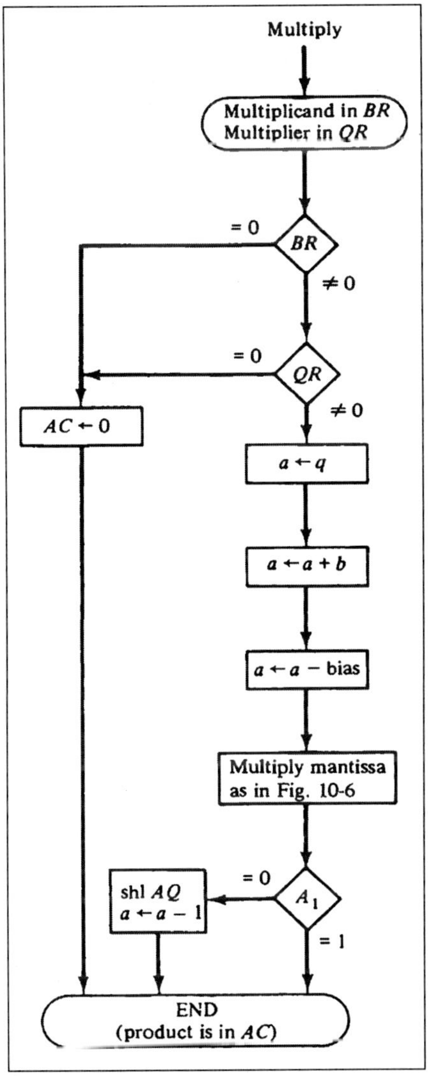

***Fig 2.13:** Multiplication of floating point numbers*

Division

The algorithm can be subdivided into five consecutive parts:

1. Check for zeros.
2. Initialize the register and evaluate the sign
3. Align the dividend
4. Subtract the exponents.
5. Divide the mantissa

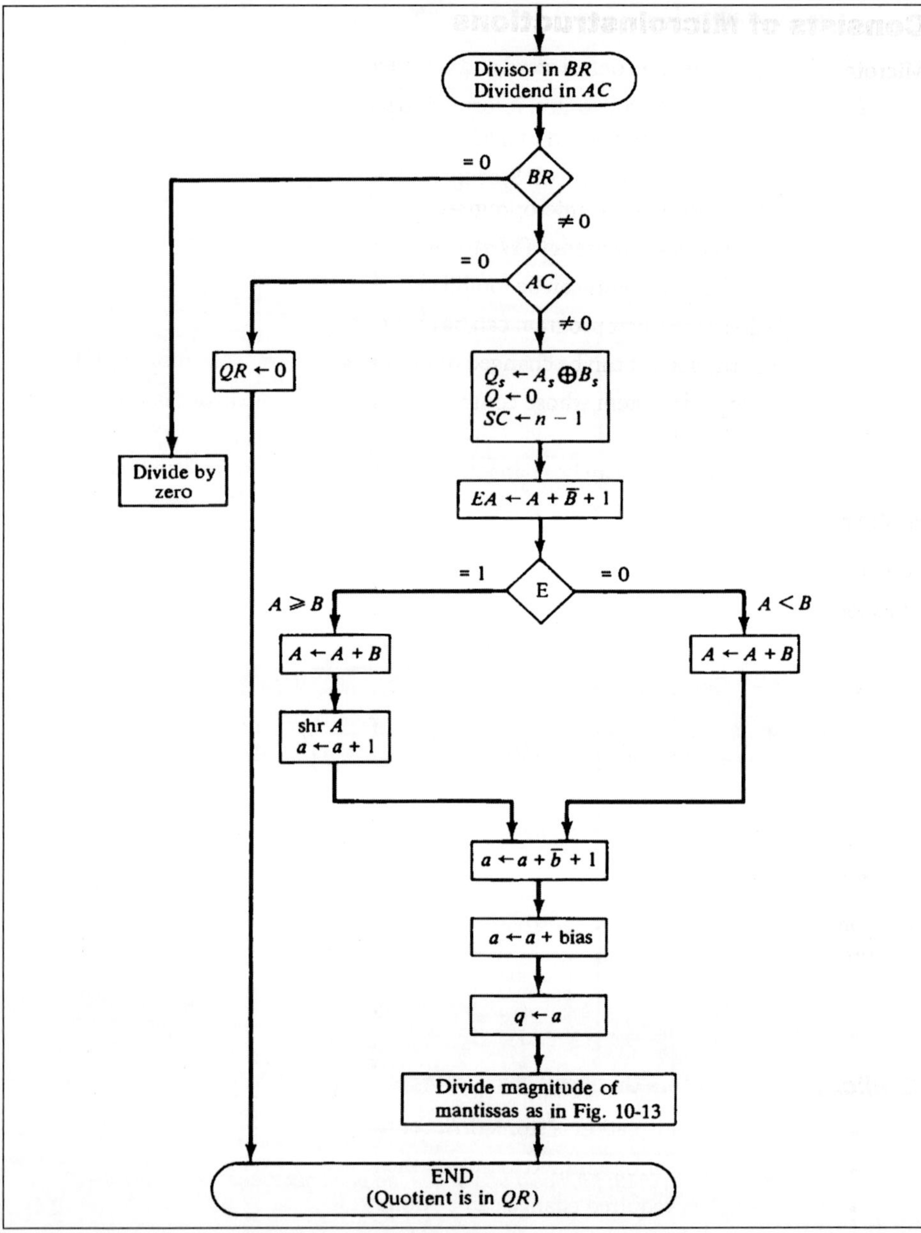

Fig 2.14: *Division of floating point numbers*

2.9 Microprogrammed Control

Microprogram

Program stored in memory that generates all the control signals required to execute the instruction set correctly

Consists of Microinstructions

Microinstruction contains a control word and a sequencing word.

- **Control Word:** All the control information required for one clock cycle Sequencing Word - Information needed to decide the next microinstruction adress
- **Control Memory (Control Storage: CS):** Storage in the microprogrammed control unit to store the microprogram.
- **Writeable Control Memory (Writeable Control Storage:WCS)**
    - CS whose contents can be modified
    - Allows the microprogram can be changed
    - Instruction set can be changed or modified Dynamic Microprogramming
    - Computer system whose control unit is implemented with a microprogram in WCS
    - Microprogram can be changed by a systems programmer or a user.

a. Control Memory

Control Unit

The Control Unit is a critical component responsible for coordinating all operations.

- **Function:** Initiate sequences of microoperations.
- **Output:** Generates Control signals (which specify microoperations) in a bus-organized system.
    - These signals are groups of bits that select the paths in multiplexers, decoders, and arithmetic logic units (ALUs).

Two Major Types of Control Unit

1. Hardwired Control

The control logic is implemented with gates, Flip-Flops (F/Fs), decoders, and other digital circuits.

- **Pros (+):** Fast operation.
- **Cons (-):** Changing the design requires a physical wiring change.

2. Microprogrammed Control

- The control information is stored in a control memory.
- This memory is programmed to initiate the required sequence of microoperations.
- **Pros (+):** Any required change can be done easily by updating the microprogram in control memory.
- **Cons (-):** Slow operation.

Control Word

The control variables at any given time can be represented by a string of 1's and 0's.

Microprogrammed Control

A control unit whose binary control variables are stored in memory (specifically, the control memory).

Microinstruction

- A Control Word stored in the Control Memory.
- The microinstruction specifies one or more microoperations.

Microprogram

- A sequence of microinstruction
- Dynamic microprogramming : *Control Memory* = RAM
    - RAM can be used for writing (*to change a writable control memory*)
- Microprogram is loaded initially from an auxiliary memory such as a magnetic disk
    - Static microprogramming : *Control Memory* = ROM

Control words in ROM are made permanent during the hardware production.

Microprogrammed Control Organization

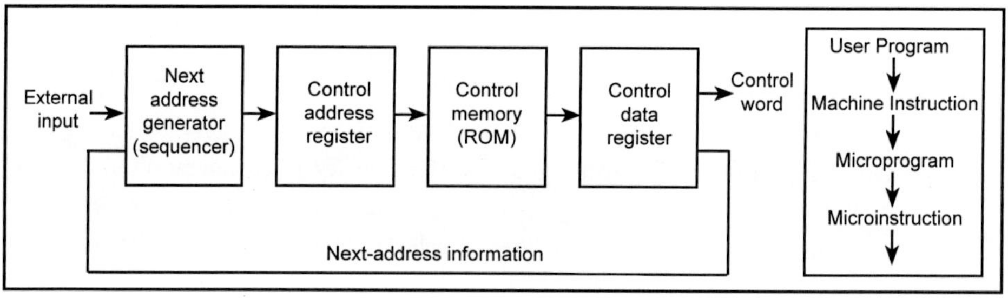

Fig 2.15: *Microprogrammed control operation*

1. Control Memory

- A memory is part of a control unit: *Microprogram*
- Computer Memory (*employs a microprogrammed control unit*)
- **Main Memory:** for storing user program (*Machine instruction/data*)
- **Control Memory:** for storing microprogram (*Microinstruction*)

2. Control Address Register

- Specify the address of the microinstruction

3. Sequencer (= Next Address Generator)

- Determine the address sequence that is read from control memory
- Next address of the next microinstruction can be specified several way depending on the sequencer input

4. Control Data Register (= Pipeline Register)

- Hold the microinstruction read from control memory

- Allows the execution of the microoperations specified by the control word
- ***simultaneously*** with the generation of the next microinstruction

b. Microprogram Example

Computer Configuration

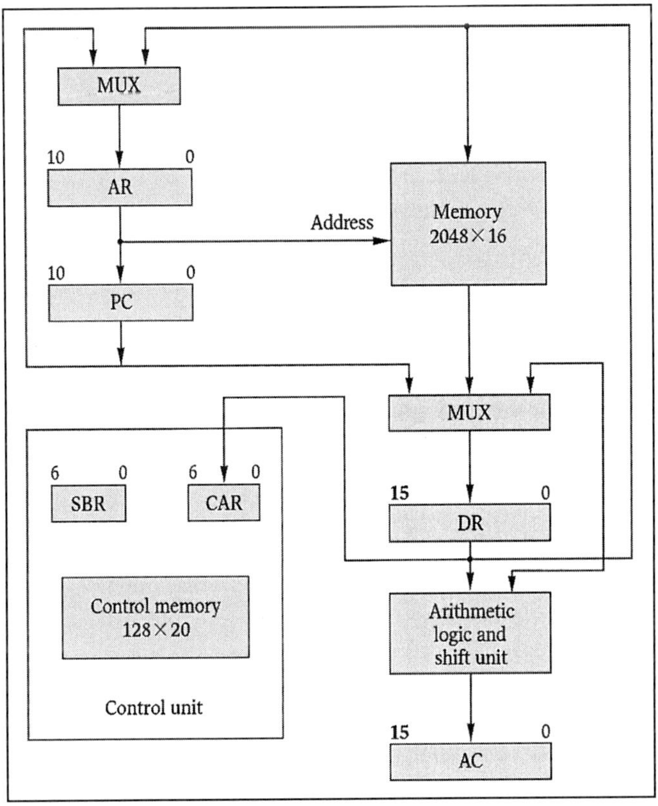

Fig 2.16: *Computer hardware configuration*

Memory

- **Main memory:** Stores *instruction* and *data.*
- **Control memory:** Stores the *microprogram.*
- **Data Transfer:**
  - Data written to memory come from DR (Data Register).
  - Data read from memory can go only to DR.

CPU Register and ALU

The main CPU components are the DR, AR, PC, AC, ALU.

- **DR (Data Register):** DR can receive information from AC, PC, or Memory (*selected by MUX*).

- **AR (Address Register):** AR can receive information from PC or DR (*selected by MUX*).
- **PC (Program Counter):** PC can receive information only from AR.
- **ALU (Arithmetic Logic Unit):** ALU performs microoperation with data from AC and DR

Control Unit Register

- SBR (Subroutine Register)
- CAR (Control Address Register)

Instruction Format

- Instruction Format: ***Fig. 2.22***

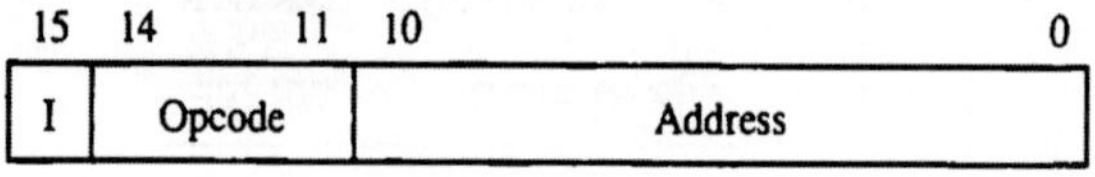

(a) Instruction format

Fig 2.17: *Computer instruction format*

- I : 1 bit for indirect addressing
- Opcode: 4 bit operation code
- Address: 11 bit address for system memory

Micro Operation Fields: F1, F2, F3

- **Width:** 3bits each (e.g., F1, F2, F3)
- **Constraint:** Two or more conflicting microoperations cannot be specified simultaneously.

Example of Conflicting Operations

- 010 001 000: This combination represents conflicting micro-operations.
- It's not possible to Clear AC to 0 and subtract DR from AC at the same time.
- Symbol DRTAC(F1 = 100): This symbol could stand for a transfer from DR to AC (AC $\leftarrow$ DR).

Condition Field (CD)

- **Width**: 2 bits.
- **Purpose:** Specifies which status bit is to be tested for a conditional branch.

CD Value	Description
00	Unconditional branch, U = 1
01	Indirect address bit, I = DR(15)
10	Sign bit of AC, S = AC(15)
11	Zero value in AC, Z = AC = 0

Address Fields (AD)

- **Width:** 7 bits.
- **Context:** AD128 word: This suggests a 128×20 bit Control Memory organization.

Table 2.5: *Symbols and binary code for microinstruction fields*

F1	Microoperation	Symbol
000	None	NOP
001	$AC \leftarrow AC + DR$	ADD
010	$AC \leftarrow 0$	CLRAC
011	$AC \leftarrow AC + 1$	INCAC
100	$AC \leftarrow DR$	DRTAC
101	$AR \leftarrow DR(0\text{–}10)$	DRTAR
110	$AR \leftarrow PC$	PCTAR
111	$M[AR] \leftarrow DR$	WRITE

F2	Microoperation	Symbol
000	None	NOP
001	$AC \leftarrow AC - DR$	SUB
010	$AC \leftarrow AC \vee DR$	OR
011	$AC \leftarrow AC \wedge DR$	AND
100	$DR \leftarrow M[AR]$	READ
101	$DR \leftarrow AC$	ACTDR
110	$DR \leftarrow DR + 1$	INCDR
111	$DR(0\text{-}10) \leftarrow PC$	PCTDR

F3	Microoperation	Symbol
000	None	NOP
001	$AC \leftarrow AC \oplus DR$	XOR
010	$AC \leftarrow \overline{AC}$	COM
011	$AC \leftarrow \text{shl } AC$	SHL
100	$AC \leftarrow \text{shr } AC$	SHR
101	$PC \leftarrow PC + 1$	INCPC
110	$PC \leftarrow AR$	ARTPC
111	Reserved	

CD	Condition	Symbol	Comments
00	Always = 1	U	Unconditional branch
01	$DR(15)$	I	Indirect address bit
10	$AC(15)$	S	Sign bit of AC
11	$AC = 0$	Z	Zero value in AC

BR	Symbol	Function
00	JMP	$CAR \leftarrow AD$ if condition = 1 $CAR \leftarrow CAR + 1$ if condition = 0
01	CALL	$CAR \leftarrow AD$, $SBR \leftarrow CAR + 1$ if condition = 1 $CAR \leftarrow CAR + 1$ if condition = 0
10	RET	$CAR \leftarrow SBR$ (Return from subroutine)
11	MAP	$CAR(2\text{–}5) \leftarrow DR(11\text{–}14)$, $CAR(0,1,6) \leftarrow 0$

Branch Field (BR)

- **Width:** 2 bits.
- **Purpose:** Specifies the type of branch operation.

BR Value	Description
00	JMP (Unconditional Jump) • Condition = 0 : • Condition = 1 :
01	CALL • Condition = 0 : • Condition = 1 :
10	RET
11	MAP
	7 bit Address Fields : AD128 word : 128 × 20 bit

2.10 Micro Programmed Control

A Microprogrammed Control Unit is a fundamental component of a computer's central processing unit (CPU) responsible for generating control signals required to execute instructions. Instead of using hardwired logic to decode instructions, a microprogrammed control unit uses a control memory containing microinstructions that dictate the sequence of operations. This approach makes the control unit more flexible, allowing modifications and extensions to the instruction set without changing hardware.

Concept of Microprogramming

Microprogramming is a method of implementing the control logic of a CPU using a **firmware-based approach**. Instead of directly generating control signals through combinational logic, a sequence of **microinstructions** stored in a **control memory (CM)** generates these signals step by step. Each machine instruction is executed by breaking it into a series of **micro-operations**, which are controlled by the microprogram.

A **microinstruction** is a low-level instruction that specifies control signals to perform basic operations like fetching operands, executing ALU operations, or writing results to registers. A sequence of microinstructions forms a **microprogram**, which corresponds to a machine instruction in the CPU's instruction set.

Structure of a Microprogrammed Control Unit

The microprogrammed control unit consists of several key components:

1. **Control Memory (CM):** Stores the microprogram (set of microinstructions).
2. **Control Address Register (CAR):** Holds the address of the current microinstruction.
3. **Control Data Register (CDR):** Temporarily holds the microinstruction fetched from control memory.
4. **Microinstruction Decoder:** Decodes the microinstruction to generate control signals.

5. **Sequencing Logic:** Determines the next microinstruction to be executed.

The control unit follows these steps during execution:

- The **CAR** fetches a microinstruction from **CM.**
- The **microinstruction decoder** translates it into control signals.
- The control signals activate the required hardware components (ALU, registers, memory).
- The **sequencing logic** determines the next microinstruction address and updates the **CAR.**

Types of Microinstructions

- Microinstructions contain fields that specify the operation to be performed. There are two primary formats:

1. Horizontal Microinstructions

- Each bit corresponds to a specific control signal.
- Multiple operations can be performed simultaneously.
- Requires more memory but offers high parallelism.

2. Vertical Microinstructions

- Uses compact encoding, where a smaller number of bits represent control signals.
- Requires decoding circuits but saves memory.
- Suitable for microprogrammed control units with limited control memory.

Microinstruction Execution Cycle

Each machine-level instruction is executed in multiple **microinstructions** stored in control memory. The typical execution cycle includes:

1. **Fetch Phase:** Fetch the microinstruction from control memory.
2. **Decode Phase:** Decode the microinstruction and generate control signals.
3. **Execute Phase:** Perform the specified micro-operations.
4. **Next Address Computation:** Determine the next microinstruction based on the instruction sequence or branching conditions.

Advantages of Microprogrammed Control Units

- **Simplifies Control Logic:** Reduces hardware complexity compared to hardwired control.
- **Flexibility:** New instructions can be added by modifying the microprogram.
- **Easier Debugging and Modifications:** Control memory can be updated to fix errors or optimize performance.
- **Standardization:** Allows for designing multiple processors with the same control unit but different instruction sets.

Disadvantages of Microprogrammed Control Units

- **Slower Execution:** Fetching and decoding microinstructions introduces delays compared to hardwired control units.

- **Increased Memory Requirement:** Requires additional storage for control memory.
- **More Complex Design:** Needs sequencing logic to manage microinstruction flow.

2.11 Design of Control Unit

The **Control Unit (CU)** is a crucial component of a computer's CPU that directs the execution of instructions by generating appropriate control signals. It interprets machine instructions, manages the flow of data within the CPU, and coordinates operations among the Arithmetic Logic Unit (ALU), memory, and input/output devices. The control unit ensures that each instruction is executed in the correct sequence and at the right time.

Functions of a Control Unit

The control unit performs the following key functions:

- **Instruction Fetching:** Retrieves the next instruction from memory.
- **Instruction Decoding:** Interprets the instruction's opcode and determines the required operations.
- **Generating Control Signals:** Activates the necessary control lines to execute the instruction.
- **Sequencing Execution:** Ensures operations occur in the correct order using a control sequence.
- **Managing Data Transfer:** Coordinates data movement between registers, ALU, and memory.
- **Handling Interrupts:** Manages interruptions from I/O devices and prioritizes execution.

Types of Control Unit Design

- The control unit can be implemented using two primary approaches:

A. Hardwired Control Unit

- Uses fixed logic circuits to generate control signals.
- Designed using combinational and sequential logic circuits.
- Fast execution speed due to direct signal generation.
- Difficult to modify or update once implemented.
- Best suited for **Reduced Instruction Set Computing (RISC)** architectures.

B. Microprogrammed Control Unit

- Uses a **control memory** to store sequences of microinstructions that generate control signals.
- Flexible and allows modification by updating the microprogram.
- Slower than hardwired control due to memory access overhead.
- Used in **Complex Instruction Set Computing (CISC)** architectures.

Basic Components of a Control Unit

- A control unit consists of several key components to manage instruction execution:
- **Instruction Register (IR):** Holds the current instruction being executed.

- **Program Counter (PC):** Tracks the address of the next instruction.
- **Decoder:** Translates instruction opcodes into control signals.
- **Timing and Control Logic:** Generates sequence signals for executing instructions.
- **Control Memory (in microprogrammed control):** Stores microinstructions that generate control signals.

Design Steps for a Control Unit

Step 1: Define the Instruction Set

- Identify the instructions the processor will support, including arithmetic, logic, memory access, and control operations.

Step 2: Identify Required Control Signals

- List all signals needed to operate the ALU, registers, memory, and buses for each instruction.

Step 3: Design the Control Logic

- Depending on the control unit type:
- **Hardwired Approach:** Use logic gates, flip-flops, and state machines to generate signals.
- **Microprogrammed Approach:** Create a control memory that stores sequences of microinstructions.

Step 4: Develop Instruction Execution Sequencing

- Define how each instruction is broken down into smaller steps:

1. **Fetch Cycle:** Retrieve instruction from memory.
2. **Decode Cycle:** Identify operation and operands.
3. **Execute Cycle:** Perform ALU or memory operations.
4. **Write-Back Cycle:** Store the result in registers or memory.

Step 5: Implement Branching and Interrupt Handling

- Ensure proper handling of conditional jumps, loops, and external interrupts for efficient program execution.

Hardwired Control Unit Design

- A **Hardwired Control Unit** uses a sequential circuit to generate control signals based on instruction opcodes. The major components include:
- **Instruction Decoder:** Decodes the opcode into a unique output.
- **State Machine:** Defines control signal sequences for each instruction.
- **Combinational Logic:** Uses logic gates to generate control signals dynamically.

Advantages of Hardwired Control

- Faster execution due to direct logic implementation.
- Efficient for simple instruction sets (RISC processors).

Disadvantages of Hardwired Control

- Complex hardware design for large instruction sets.
- Difficult to modify or add new instructions.

Microprogrammed Control Unit Design

- A **Microprogrammed Control Unit** stores control signals in a microprogram (firmware). The execution follows predefined microinstructions stored in control memory.

Components of Microprogrammed Control

- **Control Memory:** Stores microinstructions for generating control signals.
- **Control Address Register (CAR):** Holds the address of the next microinstruction.
- **Control Data Register (CDR):** Stores the microinstruction being executed.
- **Sequencer:** Determines the next microinstruction to execute.

Advantages of Microprogrammed Control

- Flexible and easy to modify by updating the microprogram.
- Supports complex instruction sets (CISC architectures).

Disadvantages of Microprogrammed Control

- Slower than hardwired control due to memory access delays.
- Requires more memory to store microinstructions

Summary

The unit begins with an introduction to the Arithmetic Logic Unit (ALU), which is responsible for executing arithmetic and logical operations in digital computers. Arithmetic operations include addition, subtraction, multiplication, and division, performed using fixed-point and floating-point representations. Logical operations manipulate binary data using AND, OR, XOR, and NOT functions. Shift operations, including logical, arithmetic, and circular shifts, facilitate data manipulation for multiplication and division.

The Arithmetic Logic Shift Unit (ALSU) integrates arithmetic, logic, and shift operations into a single component, enhancing computational efficiency. The unit also explores MIPS architecture, a Reduced Instruction Set Computing (RISC) design known for its efficiency and pipelining capabilities. MIPS instructions are categorized into R-type, I-type, and J-type formats, supporting efficient instruction execution. Additionally, the unit covers addition and subtraction for signed and unsigned numbers, utilizing algorithms such as Booth's multiplication for efficient computation. The division process is explained using binary division techniques, and floating-point arithmetic operations demonstrate how large numbers and fractional values are processed.

The unit concludes with the microprogrammed control unit, which generates control signals for executing instructions. It contrasts hardwired control units, which use fixed logic, with microprogrammed control, which employs a control memory storing microinstructions. The design of control units includes instruction fetching, decoding, execution sequencing, and branching mechanisms. This unit provides a foundation for understanding how digital systems perform arithmetic computations and execute instructions efficiently.

EXERCISES

S.No.	16 Marks Questions	Level
1	Suppose you have two binary numbers: 0110 (which is 6) by 0011 (which is 3). Use Booth's multiplication algorithm to compute their product. What is the result in binary and decimal?	L3
2	Add the following floating point numbers 1.101 × 2^3 and 0.011 × 2^2 3.25 × 2^4 and 0.5 × 2^0 1.0 × 2^1 and 0.5 × 2^0 Show the steps involved in aligning the exponents, adding the mantissas, and normalizing the result.	L4
3	Imagine you're using Booth's algorithm to multiply 0110 (which is 6 in binary) by 1001 (which is -7 in two's complement). Walk through the algorithm step-by-step and show the intermediate results for each iteration.	L5
4	Design and analyse the 8 bit adder - subtractor circuit, explain how it works and demonstrate the sequence of operations for both addition and subtraction for the following example. A=10101101 B=11001011	L6
5	Describe how a microprogrammed control unit executes a basic instruction like ADD R1, R2, R3. Explain the sequence of microinstructions and the control signals generated.	L3
6	Explain how opcodes are encoded for different types of instructions (e.g., arithmetic, logical, data transfer, control flow). Provide examples of instructions and their binary representations.	L3
7	Evaluate the effectiveness of cache memory in reducing data access time in system. Discuss the limitations of cache memory and analyze how these limitations might impact overall system performance.	L4
8	Design an optimized memory hierarchy that balances speed, cost, and storage capacity. Justify each component of your design, explaining how it meets the demands of high-performance computing.	L5

S.No.	2 Marks Questions	Level
1	Suppose you need to add the values 0101 and 0011 using a register in a micro-processor, explain the basic steps involved in performing this addition operation at the micro-operation level.	L3
2	Explain how floating point addition is performed in a system. What are the key steps involved in aligning the exponents before adding the mantissas?	L3
3	Add the 4-bit binary numbers 1111 and 0001. What is the result in binary, and what is the overflow status?	L1
4	If you add the floating-point numbers as 1.1 × 2^0 and 1.0 × 2^2, explain the normalization process and provide the resulting normalized floating-point number.	L2

5	A 4-bit register holds the value 11001. If you perform a increment operation, what will be the result stored in the register?	L1
6	Given an 8-bit binary number 10110010, perform an arithmetic shift right and arithmetic shift left by 1 positions. What is the resulting binary value? explain the answer.	L1
7	Write the signed bit representation of the following numbers. +109 -109 +43 -43	L2
8	When adding 2.0 × 2^3 and 0.5 × 2^1, how do you adjust the exponents before performing the addition?	L2
9	In an 8-bit system, add the binary numbers 11110000 and 00001111. What is the result in binary, and is there an overflow?	L1
10	A 4-bit register holds the value 0010. If you perform a decrement operation, what will be the result stored in the register?	L1
11	How does the use of an accumulator streamline arithmetic operations in a CPU's execution cycle?	L2
12	How might a micro-programmed control unit enhance the flexibility and scalability of a computer architecture?	L2
13	In what scenarios might two's complement arithmetic be preferred over other methods for representing negative numbers?	L1
14	How do the design of RISC and CISC influence software development and optimization?	L2
15	How might the choice of shift operation affect the performance of certain algorithms in computer systems?	L2
16	In what types of applications might choose floating-point arithmetic over integer arithmetic despite its potential inefficiencies?	L1

3

Memory Organization

UNIT

RATIONALE

The study of interconnection structures, interprocessor arbitration, interprocessor communication and synchronization, and cache coherence is fundamental to modern computer architecture, particularly in multiprocessor systems. Efficient interconnection structures ensure seamless communication between processors, memory, and I/O devices, optimizing performance and scalability. Arbitration mechanisms are essential for resolving conflicts when multiple processors access shared resources, ensuring fairness and efficiency. Synchronization techniques, including locks, semaphores, and message passing, prevent data inconsistency and race conditions. Cache coherence is crucial for maintaining data integrity across multiple caches, preventing stale or incorrect data from being used. Mastering these concepts is essential for designing high-performance and parallel computing systems.

OUTCOMES

This unit explains the memory hierarchy, covering primary, auxiliary, associative, cache, and virtual memory. It discusses memory management techniques and optimization strategies. Upon completion, students will:

- Understand the concept of memory hierarchy and its importance in computer performance.
- Differentiate between main memory, auxiliary memory, and their storage mechanisms.
- Explore the principles of associative memory and its applications.
- Study cache memory organization, including mapping techniques and replacement policies.
- Analyze virtual memory implementation and its role in efficient memory management.
- Evaluate the impact of memory organization on overall system performance.

3.1 Memory Hierarchy

The memory unit is a critical component of any digital computer, as it is responsible for storing programs and data. The primary memory that interacts directly with the CPU is known as the main memory. Backup storage devices are referred to as auxiliary memory. Common examples of auxiliary memory devices include magnetic disks and tapes, which are used to store system programs, large data files, and other types of backup information.

The memory hierarchy in a computer system encompasses all the storage devices, ranging from the slower but higher-capacity auxiliary memory to the faster main memory, and then to an even smaller and faster cache memory that is directly accessible by the high-speed processing unit. Figure 1 provides an overview of the components found in a typical memory hierarchy.

3.2 Main Memory

Main memory serves as the central storage unit in a computer system, providing space for storing data and programs during the operation of the computer. This memory is both large in capacity and fast in speed, enabling quick access to data for the CPU. The technology used in main memory primarily involves semiconductor-based integrated circuits. These circuits come in the form of RAM (Random Access Memory) chips, which operate in two main modes: static and dynamic.

- **Static RAM (SRAM)**: This type of memory uses internal flip-flops to store binary information. It is faster and more stable but also more expensive than dynamic RAM.
- **Dynamic RAM (DRAM)**: Unlike SRAM, DRAM stores binary data as electrical charges in capacitors. Because these charges tend to dissipate over time, DRAM requires periodic refreshing to maintain the stored data. It is less expensive than SRAM but slower.

While most of the main memory in a general-purpose computer is made up of RAM chips, a portion may be dedicated to ROM (Read-Only Memory) chips as well.

- **Read-Only Memory (ROM)**: This type of memory is used to store data that does not change during normal operation, such as system programs and tables of constants. ROM is essential for storing a special initial program called a Bootstrap loader, which is responsible for starting the computer's software when the power is turned on.

Bootstrap Loader

The Bootstrap loader is a small program stored in ROM that begins the process of loading the computer's operating system into the main memory. When the computer is powered on, the Bootstrap loader is executed, which, in turn, loads a portion of the operating system from a disk into the main memory, after which control is handed over to the operating system.

RAM and ROM Chips

RAM Chip

A typical RAM chip is designed to communicate with the CPU via a bidirectional data bus with three-state buffers. The memory in this chip is organized to hold 128 words, with each word consisting of eight bits (1 byte). To access a specific word, a 7-bit address is required, and the data bus is 8 bits wide. The RAM chip also has control inputs, including the "read" (RD) and "write" (WR) lines, which dictate the memory operation.

There are two chip-select inputs (CS1 and CS2), which control whether the chip is active or not. The chip is enabled when CS1 is set to 1 and CS2 to 0. If these conditions are met, the memory can operate in either read or write mode:

- When the WR line is active, data from the data bus is written to the memory location specified by the address input.
- When the RD line is active, the data from the selected memory location is transferred onto the data bus.

If the chip select inputs are not enabled, or if the read/write operations are not active, the data bus enters a high-impedance state, effectively isolating the memory from the system.

ROM Chip

A ROM chip operates similarly to the RAM chip in terms of its external organization, but with key differences due to its read-only nature. Since ROM is designed to only provide data for reading, the data bus can only function in an output mode, unlike the bidirectional bus of RAM. The ROM chip typically has nine address lines, which allow the selection of any one of the 512 bytes of data stored in the ROM. For the ROM to operate, the chip-select inputs must be set to CS1 − 1 and CS2 = 0. If these conditions are not met, the data bus will remain in a high-impedance state, and the ROM chip will not be accessible. Thus, while RAM and ROM chips share similarities in structure, their functions and capabilities differ, with RAM supporting both reading and writing, while ROM is strictly for reading data.

Memory Address Map

The connection between the memory and the processor is established based on the required memory size and the types of RAM and ROM chips available in the system. This interconnection is facilitated through a memory address map, which is a structured table that outlines how the memory address space is assigned to different memory components. The memory address map serves as a clear, visual representation, showing the allocated memory addresses for each chip within the system.

This map is essential for the proper functioning of the computer system, as it helps in determining where each type of memory—whether RAM or ROM—is located within the overall addressable space. The memory address map also ensures that the processor can access the appropriate chip based on the address provided by the memory.

Example of a Memory Address Map

In the memory address map for a typical configuration, you will find several columns, each providing specific information:

- **Component Column**: This column identifies the type of memory chip, such as RAM or ROM, that is being used in the system.
- **Hexadecimal Address Column**: Here, a range of hexadecimal addresses is assigned to each memory chip. These addresses represent the memory locations that are mapped to the specific chip, allowing the processor to access data from the correct location.
- **Address Bus Lines Column**: This column lists the number of address lines required to uniquely identify each memory location. For example, a RAM chip with a capacity of 128 bytes will require 7 address lines (since 128 bytes require a total of 7 bits to address), while a ROM chip with a capacity of 512 bytes will require 9 address lines.

This memory address map is crucial for the efficient and accurate allocation of memory space, helping the system manage its resources and ensuring smooth communication between the processor and the various memory chips.

Memory Connection to the CPU

In a computer system, RAM (Random Access Memory) and ROM (Read-Only Memory) are linked to the CPU through two crucial buses: the data bus and the address bus. The address bus plays a key role in selecting specific memory locations. The lower-order bits of the address bus determine the exact byte within a memory chip, while the higher-order address lines help identify which memory chip should be activated by using chip select inputs.

Each RAM chip receives the seven least significant bits from the address bus, allowing it to access one of 128 possible memory locations within the chip. However, to determine which specific RAM chip should be active at any given time, address lines 8 and 9 are processed through a 2×4 decoder. This decoder generates signals that control the Chip Select (CS1) inputs of the RAM chips.

- When address lines 8 and 9 hold the binary value 00, the first RAM chip is selected.
- When the value is 01, the second RAM chip is chosen, and so on.

The Read (RD) and Write (WR) control signals generated by the microprocessor are also connected to the RAM chips, ensuring data can be read from or written to the appropriate memory locations as needed.

The system distinguishes between RAM and ROM using address bus line 10:

- If the bit on this line is 0, the system enables the RAM chips for read/write operations.
- If the bit is 1, the ROM chip is selected instead.

Unlike RAM, which allows bidirectional data transfer (both reading and writing), ROM is designed to function as a read-only memory module. Thus, its data bus is configured for output operations only, meaning it can send data to the CPU but not receive new data for storage.

Additionally, address lines 1 to 9 are directly connected to the ROM chip without passing through the decoder, ensuring a seamless address selection mechanism for reading stored instructions or data.

This setup effectively organizes memory allocation in a structured way, allowing the CPU to efficiently access both RAM and ROM based on the given address and control signals.

3.3 Auxiliary Memory and Content-Addressable Memory (CAM)

In traditional memory systems, data is retrieved based on a specific memory address, meaning the CPU must know the exact location where the information is stored. However, this method can sometimes be inefficient, especially when searching for specific data within a large dataset. A more advanced approach to memory access involves identifying and retrieving stored data based on its content rather than its physical address. This specialized type of memory is known as associative memory **or** content-addressable memory (CAM).

Features of Content-Addressable Memory (CAM)

1. Content-Based Access

Unlike conventional RAM, where data retrieval requires specifying a memory address, CAM allows the CPU to search for data using its actual content. This enables significantly faster searches since all memory locations are checked simultaneously in parallel rather than sequentially.

2. Parallel Search Capability

CAM is designed to compare stored data against a given search value in a single operation, rather than scanning through memory locations one by one. This simultaneous search process makes CAM highly efficient for applications like network routing, database management, and cache memory systems.

3. Higher Cost and Complexity

Associative memory is **more expensive than standard RAM** because each memory cell is not only responsible for storing data but must also include additional logic circuits for performing comparisons. This added complexity increases manufacturing costs and power consumption, making CAM less commonly used in general-purpose computing but highly valuable in specialized applications.

Key Components of CAM

Argument Register

The argument register is used to hold an external search argument (or query) that is compared against the content stored in CAM. When a match is found, the memory unit retrieves the corresponding data.

Key Register

The key register acts as a mask that allows selective searching within specific fields of the argument word. This means that only certain portions of the stored data are considered during the comparison process, making searches more flexible and efficient.

3.4 Hardware Organization of Associative Memory

The hardware organization of an associative memory system consists of a memory array along with specialized logic circuits designed to process data efficiently. The system is structured to handle m words, each containing n bits. Unlike conventional memory, which retrieves data based on specific addresses, associative memory performs parallel searches, enabling faster data retrieval.

Key Components of Associative Memory Hardware

1. Memory Array

The core component of associative memory is the memory array, where data is stored. Each word in this array consists of **n bits**, allowing the system to store and compare multiple words simultaneously.

2. Argument Register (A)

The argument register holds an external search query, which consists of **n bits**—one for each bit position in a memory word. This register plays a crucial role in the content-based search process by providing the data pattern that needs to be matched against the stored words.

3. Key Register (K)

The key register is another n-bit register that serves as a mask to selectively choose which bit positions in the argument register should be considered during the comparison process.

By using the key register, the system can perform searches based on partial matches rather than requiring an exact match for all bits in a word.

4. Match Register (M)

The match register consists of m bits, with each bit corresponding to one memory word. When a search operation is performed, every word in the memory array is compared in parallel with the contents of the argument register. If a word matches the bit pattern in the argument register (as determined by the key register), the corresponding bit in the match register is set to 1. Words that do not match remain unset (0).

Matching and Data Retrieval Process

- The memory system performs a parallel search by comparing each stored word against the argument register simultaneously.
- The match register records which words successfully matched the search criteria.
- After the comparison process, the set bits in the match register indicate which memory words meet the search condition.
- To retrieve the matched words, the system performs a sequential access to memory, fetching only those words that correspond to the set bits in the match register.

This hardware organization allows associative memory to quickly locate and retrieve data based on content rather than address, making it highly effective for applications requiring fast lookups, such as database indexing, cache memory, and high-speed networking.

Read and Write Operations in Associative Memory

In associative memory, data retrieval and storage are managed through read and write operations that enable fast content-based searches. The process relies on parallel comparison and match registers to determine which memory words correspond to a given search argument.

Read Operation

During a read operation, the system searches for words that match a given argument stored in the argument register. The retrieval process follows these steps:

1. Identifying Matching Words

- Each bit in the argument register is compared to the corresponding bits in all memory words simultaneously.
- If a word matches the argument (considering the unmasked bits specified by the key register), the corresponding bit in the match register (M) is set to 1.
- If multiple words match, multiple bits in the match register will be set.

2. Reading Matched Words

- The system applies a read signal to each memory word whose corresponding match register bit (M_1) is set to 1.
- This allows the matched words to be retrieved sequentially, ensuring efficient data access.

3. Handling Unique Entries

- In cases where the memory does not store duplicate items, only one word will match a given search argument.
- When this happens, the M_1 output can be used directly as a read signal for that word, making the retrieval process even more efficient.

Understanding the Memory Array and External Registers

The structure of associative memory consists of a memory array, where each cell in the array is labeled as C_{ij}:

- i represents the word number (or row).
- j represents the bit position in the word (or column).

Each bit A_j in the argument register is compared with all bits in the j-th column of the memory array, provided that the key register (K) allows it ($K_j = 1$).

- This comparison is performed for all columns (j = 1, 2, ... n).
- If all unmasked bits in a memory word match the argument, the corresponding bit M_1 in the match register is set to 1.
- If even one bit does not match, M_1 is cleared to 0, indicating no match.

Write Operation

A write operation in associative memory involves storing a new bit in the memory cell. Each memory cell consists of:

- A flip-flop storage element (F_{ij}) that holds the bit.
- Circuitry for reading, writing, and matching stored data.

Steps in a Write Operation

1. Transferring Input Data

- The new bit is written into the appropriate storage cell (F_{ij}).
- This ensures that the data is stored correctly and is available for future comparisons.

2. Retrieving Stored Data

- When a read operation is performed, the bit stored in F_{ij} is retrieved and sent to the output.

3. Matching Process

- During a search operation, the match logic compares the content of F_{ij} with the corresponding bit in the argument register.
- If the bit matches the search criteria (as determined by the key register), the decision logic sets the match register bit (M_1) to 1.
- Otherwise, the match register remains 0, indicating no match.

3.5 Cache Memory

In modern computing systems, cache memory plays a crucial role in bridging the speed gap between the central processing unit (CPU) and main memory. The efficiency of cache memory is based on a fundamental characteristic of computer programs known as the locality of reference.

This principle states that, at any given time, memory accesses tend to be concentrated within a small set of memory locations, rather than being spread randomly across the entire address space.

Locality of Reference: The Key to Cache Efficiency

1. Concentrated Memory Access

- Memory references in a program are often clustered within specific regions for extended periods.
- This is because programs frequently execute loops, nested loops, and function calls, which repeatedly access the same set of instructions and data.

2. Frequent Reuse of Instructions and Data

- Certain sections of a program are executed multiple times during its run, while other portions are accessed much less frequently.
- The repeated use of localized program instructions over short intervals is what makes cache memory effective.

Role of Cache Memory in System Performance

A high-speed cache memory is strategically placed between the CPU and main memory to store frequently accessed program instructions and data. Since cache access time is much closer to the CPU's clock cycle time, it helps reduce memory access delays, which are otherwise limited by the slower main memory.

- Cache stores segments of programs currently being executed and temporary data needed for computations.
- The cache compensates for the speed difference between the CPU and main memory, ensuring that the processor does not remain idle while waiting for data to be fetched.

Cache Memory Organization and Functioning

Memory Storage and Addressing

- The main memory in a system can typically store a large amount of data (e.g., 32K words, each 12 bits in size).
- However, cache memory is much smaller, holding only a subset of main memory at any given time (e.g., 512 words).
- Each word stored in cache has a duplicate copy in main memory, ensuring consistency between the two storage levels.
- When the CPU requests a memory word, it first checks the cache.
  - If the word is found in cache (cache hit), it is accessed directly from there.
  - If the word is not in cache (cache miss), it is retrieved from main memory and loaded into cache for future reference.

Cache Memory Operations

Read Operations

1. Cache Hit (Data Found in Cache)

- When the CPU makes a read request, the cache controller checks whether the requested word is already present in cache.
- If the requested data is found, it is directly read from cache without involving main memory, significantly reducing access time.

2. Cache Miss (Data Not Found in Cache)

- If the requested word is not found in cache, it results in a read miss.
- Two possible strategies are used to fetch data:
  - **Load Through (Block Fetching)**: The entire block of words containing the requested data is transferred from main memory to cache, and the CPU accesses the word from cache.
  - **Early Restart**: The requested word is sent directly to the CPU first, and then the cache is updated in parallel.

Write Operations

1. Cache Hit (Data Found in Cache)

- When the CPU writes data to a memory address that exists in cache, it updates the cache first.
- Two approaches are used for synchronizing data between cache and main memory:
  - **Write Through**: Both cache and main memory are updated simultaneously.
  - **Write Back (Copy Back)**: Only the cache is updated initially, and the main memory is updated later when the cache block is replaced. This method reduces unnecessary memory writes.

2. Cache Miss (Data Not Found in Cache)

- If the requested memory word is not in cache, a write miss occurs.
- The system fetches the required block from main memory and updates the cache before performing the write operation.

Mapping and Replacement Strategies

Mapping Function: Associating Main Memory Blocks with Cache Blocks

- The number of blocks in cache is much smaller than in main memory.
- A mapping function determines how blocks in main memory correspond to blocks in cache to efficiently manage data storage and retrieval.

Replacement Algorithm: Managing Cache Space

- When cache is full and a new block needs to be loaded, the system must decide which existing block to remove.

- The replacement algorithm follows predefined rules for selecting which cache block to evict and replace.
- Common strategies include:
  - **Least Recently Used (LRU):** The least recently accessed block is replaced.
  - **First In, First Out (FIFO):** The oldest block in cache is replaced.
  - **Random Replacement:** A block is randomly selected for replacement.

Memory Mapping Functions: Efficient Data Retrieval in CacheMemory

Memory mapping functions are essential in determining how blocks of main memory are mapped into cache memory. These functions define the correspondence between main memory blocks and cache blocks, optimizing data retrieval speed and ensuring efficient memory utilization. There are three primary techniques used in memory mapping:

1. Direct Mapping
2. Associative Mapping
3. Set-Associative Mapping

1. Direct Mapping: Simple but Rigid Allocation

Direct mapping follows a fixed allocation approach where each block of main memory is mapped to a specific block in the cache. This rigid mapping makes it easy to locate data but limits flexibility in cache utilization.

Address Division in Direct Mapping

- The CPU address consists of 15 bits, which are divided into two fields:
- Index Field (9 bits): Determines the specific cache block where data will be placed.
- Tag Field (6 bits): Identifies which main memory block is stored in the indexed cache location.
- The index bits are used to access a specific location in the cache.
- The tag bits are stored along with the data when a word is loaded into the cache.

Cache Access Mechanism

1. When the CPU generates a memory request, the index field is used to locate the corresponding cache block.
2. The tag bits from the CPU address are then compared with the tag bits stored in the cache.
3. If the tags match → It results in a cache hit, and data is retrieved directly from the cache.
4. If the tags do not match → A cache miss occurs, and the requested word is fetched from main memory and stored in the corresponding cache block.

Advantages of Direct Mapping

✓ Simple hardware implementation

✓ Fast lookup due to direct indexing

Disadvantages of Direct Mapping

✗ **Limited flexibility:** Each memory block can only be stored in one specific cache location, increasing cache conflicts.

✗ Frequent cache misses due to rigid mapping.

2. Associative Mapping: Flexible but Costly

Unlike direct mapping, associative mapping allows any block of main memory to be stored in any cache block. This increases flexibility but requires complex hardware to manage the lookup process.

Cache Structure in Associative Mapping

- The cache stores both the memory address (tag) and data together.
- The CPU searches for a matching memory address within the cache before fetching the data.

Cache Access Mechanism

1. When the CPU sends a 15-bit address, it is placed in the argument register.
2. The cache is searched in parallel to find a matching address tag.
3. If a match is found, the corresponding 12-bit data word is sent to the CPU (cache hit).
4. If no match occurs, the requested word is fetched from main memory (cache miss) and stored in cache.

Advantages of Associative Mapping

✓ Flexible storage – Any memory block can be placed anywhere in the cache.

✓ Minimizes cache misses since data is not restricted to a single location.

Disadvantages of Associative Mapping

✗ Expensive hardware – Requires additional logic for searching and comparing addresses.

✗ Increased access time due to parallel searches across the cache.

3. Set-Associative Mapping: A Balanced Approach

Set-associative mapping combines the features of both direct and associative mapping. It offers a balance between flexibility and efficiency by dividing cache into sets, where each memory block can be placed in any block within a specific set.

Cache Structure in Set-Associative Mapping

- The cache is divided into multiple sets, with each set containing a fixed number of blocks (e.g., 2-way, 4-way).
- Each memory block can be placed in any block within a designated set instead of a specific cache block.

Cache Access Mechanism

1. When the CPU generates an address, the index field is used to identify the set where the data might be stored.
2. The tag field of the CPU address is compared with all the tags in the identified set.
3. If a match is found, the corresponding data word is retrieved (cache hit).

4. If no match is found (cache miss), the requested memory word is fetched from main memory and stored in the set, replacing an existing block based on a replacement algorithm.

Advantages of Set-Associative Mapping

✓ Better flexibility than direct mapping – Multiple blocks can be stored in each set.

✓ Lower hardware cost compared to associative mapping – Only a subset of cache is searched.

✓ Reduces cache conflicts compared to direct mapping.

Disadvantages of Set-Associative Mapping

✗ More complex hardware than direct mapping – Requires multiple comparisons per set.

✗ Not as flexible as fully associative mapping, but offers a good trade-off.

Choosing the Right Cache Mapping Technique Depends on the System Requirements

- Direct Mapping is simple and fast but may result in frequent cache misses.
- Associative Mapping offers maximum flexibility but is costly and complex.
- Set-Associative Mapping provides a good balance between efficiency, cost, and performance.

By implementing the right mapping function, a system can optimize memory access times, improve cache utilization, and enhance overall processing efficiency.

Cache Replacement Policies: Efficient Memory Management

When the cache memory is full and new data needs to be loaded, a decision must be made about which existing data should be removed. This decision-making process is governed by replacement policies, which determine which cache block should be evicted to make space for the new data. The choice of replacement policy depends largely on the mapping technique used in the cache memory organization.

1. Replacement Policy in Direct Mapping

- In direct mapping, each block of main memory is mapped to a specific cache block.
- Since only one possible location exists for any given memory block, no replacement policy is required.
- Whenever a new block is loaded, it automatically replaces the previous block stored in the same cache location.
- This approach is simple but can lead to frequent cache misses if the same location is repeatedly overwritten.

2. Replacement Policies in Associative Mapping

In associative mapping, a memory block can be placed anywhere in the cache. This flexibility means that when the cache is full, an appropriate replacement policy is needed to select which block to remove. Some common strategies include:

First-In, First-Out (FIFO) Replacement Policy

- The oldest stored data is removed first when new data needs to be inserted.
- Works in a round-robin manner, where cache blocks are replaced in the order they were added.
- Simple to implement, but may not always be optimal, as the oldest data is not necessarily the least useful.

3. Replacement Policies in Set-Associative Mapping

Since set-associative mapping allows a memory block to be placed in any block within a specific set, replacement policies are necessary when all blocks within a set are occupied. The following strategies are commonly used:

1. Random Replacement Policy

- A randomly chosen block within the set is replaced when a new block is loaded.
- Simple implementation, but it does not consider which blocks are frequently accessed, potentially leading to unnecessary cache misses.

2. First-In, First-Out (FIFO) Replacement Policy

- The oldest block in the set is removed first.
- Blocks are maintained in a queue, and when a new block is loaded, the first block in the queue is evicted.
- Easy to manage, but like FIFO in associative mapping, it does not consider the actual usage frequency of the data.

3. Least Recently Used (LRU) Replacement Policy

- The block that has been used the least recently is replaced.
- The CPU keeps track of cache accesses, and when a replacement is needed, the least recently accessed block is evicted.
- More effective than FIFO because it retains frequently used data, reducing cache misses.
- However, hardware implementation is complex, requiring additional logic to track access history.

3.6 Virtual Memory

Virtual memory is a memory management technique that allows a computer system to use secondary storage (such as a hard drive or SSD) as an extension of main memory (RAM). This technique enables programs to execute as if they have access to a much larger memory space than what is physically available. In virtual memory, the addresses used by a program (virtual addresses) differ from the actual physical addresses used by the system to store data. The memory management unit (MMU) is responsible for automatically translating these virtual addresses into corresponding physical addresses. The maximum size of virtual memory is determined by the addressing capability of the computer system and the amount of secondary storage available, rather than being limited by the actual RAM capacity.

How Virtual Memory Works

Virtual memory is implemented through a combination of hardware and software. It relies on address translation mechanisms that map a program's virtual addresses to physical memory locations dynamically.

Key Characteristics of Virtual Memory

1. *Logical Addressing*

- Every process works with logical addresses that are translated into physical addresses at runtime.
- This allows processes to be moved within memory, enhancing system flexibility.

2. *Non-Contiguous Memory Allocation*

- Unlike traditional memory allocation, virtual memory allows a process to be stored in non-contiguous locations.
- This eliminates the need for programs to be loaded as a single continuous block, reducing memory fragmentation.

3. *Swapping & Paging Mechanism*

- A process does not need to reside entirely in RAM for execution.
- Swapping allows inactive parts of a program to be stored in secondary storage and brought back to RAM when needed.
- This enables multiple programs to run simultaneously without exhausting RAM.

4. *Use of Page Tables & Segment Tables*

- Address translation is managed through page tables (for paging systems) or segment tables (for segmentation-based systems).
- These tables store mappings between virtual and physical addresses, ensuring smooth memory access.

Implementation Techniques of Virtual Memory

1. *Demand Paging*

- The most common method of implementing virtual memory.
- Divides programs into fixed-size pages, which are loaded into memory only when needed.
- When a program accesses a page that is not in RAM, a page fault occurs, prompting the system to fetch the required page from secondary storage.

2. *Segmentation*

- Instead of fixed-sized pages, memory is divided into variable-sized segments, each corresponding to logical parts of a program (e.g., functions, arrays, or objects).
- Allows programs to be structured logically, reducing fragmentation and improving memory utilization.

3. Demand Segmentation

- A hybrid approach that combines demand paging and segmentation to provide greater flexibility.
- Segments are divided into pages, and pages are loaded into RAM only when necessary.

Advantages of Virtual Memory

✓ Efficient Memory Utilization – Allows multiple processes to run concurrently without requiring them to fully reside in RAM.

✓ Eliminates External Fragmentation – Non-contiguous allocation prevents unused memory gaps.

✓ Improved Process Isolation & Security – Each process operates within its own virtual address space, enhancing security and preventing conflicts.

Summary

Interconnection structures define how processors, memory, and peripherals communicate in a system. These structures include bus-based architectures, crossbar switches, and multistage networks, each offering different trade-offs in speed, scalability, and complexity. Effective interprocessor arbitration ensures that multiple processors can fairly access shared resources, using centralized or distributed arbitration techniques. Communication between processors is achieved through shared memory or message passing, while synchronization mechanisms such as locks, barriers, and spinlocks prevent race conditions and ensure proper execution order. Cache coherence is a critical challenge in multiprocessor systems, requiring protocols like MESI to maintain data consistency across multiple caches. When multiple processors access the same data, coherence protocols determine how updates propagate to prevent inconsistencies. Without proper coherence management, outdated or incorrect data may lead to computation errors. Efficient cache management techniques such as write-through and write-back policies enhance system performance by reducing memory access latency. Understanding these topics is essential for designing efficient multi-core processors, distributed computing systems, and high-performance computing architectures. Mastery of these concepts allows architects to build scalable, high-speed computing environments that maximize processing power while maintaining data consistency and synchronization, ensuring efficient execution of parallel and distributed workloads.

EXERCISES

S.No.	16 Marks Questions	Level
1	Outline the key characteristics and functions of each level in the memory hierarchy. How does each type of memory contribute to overall system performance?	L4
2	Explain the concept of the memory hierarchy in computer systems. How do the different levels of memory interact with each other to provide efficient data storage and retrieval?	L3
3	Compare and contrast Cache Memory and Associative Memory in terms of their structure, usage, and impact on system performance.	L4
4	Analyze the role of virtual memory in modern operating systems. How does it complement physical memory, and what are the potential drawbacks of relying heavily on virtual memory?	L5
5	Evaluate the effectiveness of cache memory in reducing the time taken to access data. What are the limitations of cache memory, and how do these affect overall system performance?	L4
6	Design an optimized memory hierarchy for a high-performance computing system. Consider factors like speed, cost, and storage capacity in your design, and justify each choice made.	L6
7	Identify the challenges associated with managing main and auxiliary memory for applications that handle large datasets. What strategies can be employed to overcome these challenges and enhance overall system performance?	L2
8	Discuss the function of Secondary Memory in data storage and explain how it works in conjunction with Main Memory within a computer system.	L4

S.No.	2 Marks Questions	CO	Level
1	Given a scenario where a system has 8 GB of main memory, determine the impact of running a program that requires 10 GB of memory.	CO3	L2
2	Explain how virtual memory extends the physical memory of a system.	CO3	L3
3	Design a simple model that demonstrates the use of associative memory in a caching system.	CO3	L6
4	Compare and contrast the roles of cache memory and main memory in the memory hierarchy.	CO3	L4
5	List the levels of memory hierarchy from fastest to slowest data access.	CO3	L2
6	How does virtual memory support multitasking in modern operating systems?	CO3	L2

S.No.	2 Marks Questions	CO	Level
7	A computer system is experiencing slowdowns when running several applications simultaneously. Apply the concept of virtual memory to explain how it can help alleviate this issue.	CO3	L4
8	How does associative memory improve search efficiency in databases?	CO3	L2
9	A web application is designed to quickly retrieve user profiles based on unique identifiers. How does the use of associative memory enhance the efficiency of this process?	CO3	L2
10	Consider a situation where a program experiences a high number of cache misses. Analyze the potential reasons for this issue and suggest how cache optimization could improve performance.	CO3	L4
11	How does cache memory help reduce latency in accessing frequently used data?	CO3	L2
12	Give one example of an application where associative memory is useful.	CO3	L2
13	In a scenario where a program uses a large array, analyze how insufficient main memory would impact the program's execution speed and performance.	CO3	L2
14	How does auxiliary memory differ from main memory in terms of speed and storage capacity?	CO3	L2
15	How does the memory hierarchy improve system performance?	CO3	L2
16	A software application crashes when trying to process a large dataset, indicating insufficient memory. How does this scenario illustrate the importance of main memory in computing?	CO3	L2

Input-Output Organization

4 UNIT

RATIONALE

The study of input-output (I/O) organization is crucial for understanding how a computer system communicates with external devices. Efficient I/O management ensures smooth data transfer between peripherals and the CPU, optimizing system performance. Peripheral devices, such as storage units, printers, and display screens, require proper interfacing to communicate effectively with the processor. Various data transfer techniques, including programmed I/O, interrupt-driven I/O, and direct memory access (DMA), help balance the CPU workload. Understanding priority interrupts allows for better handling of multiple I/O requests, while serial communication mechanisms ensure reliable data exchange across different devices. Mastery of these concepts is essential for efficient system design.

OUTCOMES

This unit covers the organization and management of I/O devices, various transfer modes, and the importance of priority interrupt handling. It also explores Direct Memory Access (DMA) and serial communication. After studying this unit, students will:

- Understand the classification and functions of peripheral devices in a computing system.
- Learn the importance of I/O interfaces in establishing communication between the CPU and external devices.
- Differentiate between different modes of transfer, including programmed I/O, interrupt-driven I/O, and DMA.
- Examine priority interrupt handling techniques for efficient CPU operations.
- Gain insights into the role of the Input-Output Processor (IOP) in system communication.
- Explore serial communication mechanisms and their advantages in data transmission.

4.1 Peripherals Devices

Peripherals are the input and output devices connected to a computer to expand its functionality. These devices facilitate interaction with the system, allowing users to input data and receive output.

Examples of peripheral devices include:

- **Input devices:** Keyboard, mouse
- **Output devices:** Display unit, printer
- **Storage devices:** Hard drives, magnetic disks, tapes

Types of Peripheral Devices

1. Auxiliary Storage Devices

- **Magnetic Tapes:** Used for storing large volumes of data in sequential order.
  - **Access Method:** Sequential
  - **Speed:** Slowest but most cost-effective
  - **Removability:** Can be taken out when not in use
- **Magnetic Disks:** Used for storing programs and data in bulk.
  - **Access Method:** Uses a read/write mechanism to locate data on a magnetized surface
  - **Storage:** More efficient and faster than tapes

2. Printers

Printers provide a hard copy of computer-generated text and images. There are three main types of printers:

1. **Daisy Wheel Printer:** Produces high-quality text using a print wheel but is slow.
2. **Dot Matrix Printer:** Uses a series of tiny dots to form characters, making it cost-effective but lower in quality.
3. **Laser Printer:** Delivers high-quality prints using laser technology and is commonly used in offices.

Understanding ASCII (American Standard Code for Information Interchange)

ASCII is a character encoding standard used in computers for text representation. It consists of 7-bit codes, but since most computers process 8-bit bytes, ASCII characters are often stored with one character per byte.

4.2 Input-Output (I/O) Interface

An I/O interface acts as a communication bridge between a computer's internal storage and external input/output devices. Since peripherals operate differently from the CPU, they require specialized interface units to manage data transfer and synchronization.

Challenges in Peripheral Communication

1. **Different Operating Mechanisms:** Peripherals function using electromechanical or electromagnetic processes, whereas CPUs and memory use purely electronic operations.
2. **Slower Data Transfer Rates:** The CPU processes data much faster than most peripherals.
3. **Varied Operating Modes:** Different peripherals have unique methods of operation, requiring specialized handling.
4. **Incompatible Data Formats:** Peripherals use distinct data codes and formats that may not match the CPU's word format.

I/O Bus and Interface Modules

The communication between the processor and several peripherals through the I/O Bus is shown in the following figure.

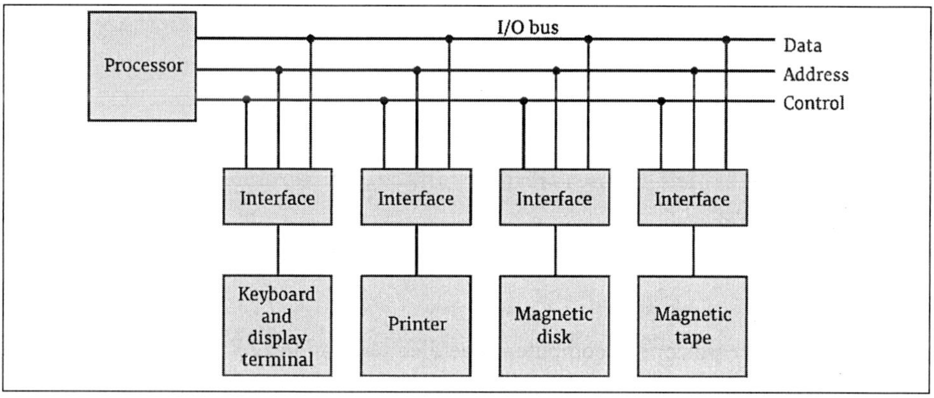

Fig 4.1: I/O Bus and Interface Modules

I/O Commands and Communication in Computer Systems

An I/O command is a function code executed within an interface to manage communication between the computer and a connected peripheral device. These commands control operations, monitor system status, and handle data transfer.

Types of I/O Commands

An interface can receive and execute four types of commands:

1. **Control Command:** Activates the peripheral device and instructs it on what operation to perform.
2. **Status Command:** Checks various conditions in the interface and peripheral to ensure proper functionality.
3. **Data Input Command:** Retrieves data from a peripheral and stores it in the interface's buffer register.
4. **Data Output Command:** Transfers data from the system bus into one of the interface registers, sending it to the connected peripheral.

I/O Bus vs. Memory Bus

There are three primary ways in which a computer can manage communication between memory and I/O devices:

1. **Separate Buses:** One bus is dedicated to memory operations, while another handles I/O functions.
2. **Shared Bus with Separate Control Lines:** A single bus is used for both memory and I/O operations, but with distinct control signals for each.
3. **Shared Bus with Common Control Lines:** A single bus is used for both memory and I/O, and the same control signals manage both functions.

Isolated I/O vs. Memory-Mapped I/O

Computers use two different methods to address I/O devices:

1. Isolated I/O

- The CPU has distinct input and output instructions specifically for I/O operations.
- Memory and I/O devices have separate address spaces and cannot overlap.
- Dedicated control signals distinguish between memory access and I/O access.

2. Memory-Mapped I/O

- There are no specialized input/output instructions; standard memory instructions handle data transfer.
- Memory and I/O share the same address space, meaning peripherals are treated like memory locations.
- Since memory and I/O addresses are unified, it simplifies hardware design but may reduce available memory addresses.

Both methods have their advantages—Isolated I/O offers clear separation between memory and peripherals, while Memory-Mapped I/O simplifies programming by treating peripherals like memory locations.

Asynchronous Data Transfer

In asynchronous data transfer, control signals are exchanged between two communicating units to coordinate the timing of data transmission.

- A strobe pulse is sent by one unit to signal the other when the data transfer should take place.
- The receiving unit then sends a response signal to confirm that the data has been successfully received.

This process, where two independent units coordinate the transfer using control signals, is known as handshaking.

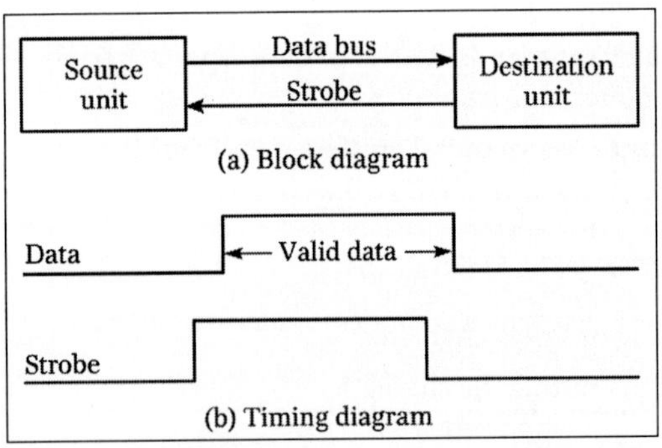

Fig 4.2: Asynchronous data transfer

Disadvantage of the Strobe Method

One major drawback of the strobe method is that the unit initiating the transfer (either the source or destination) has no way to confirm whether the data has actually been received by the other unit.

Handshaking Mechanism

Handshaking uses two control signals:

- **Data Valid:** Generated by the source unit to indicate that data is available on the bus.
- **Data Accepted:** Generated by the destination unit to confirm that the data has been received.

Handshaking Process

1. The source unit places data on the bus and activates the data valid signal.
2. The destination unit acknowledges receipt by activating the data accepted signal.
3. Once the data is received, the source unit deactivates the data valid signal, making the data on the bus invalid.
4. The destination unit then deactivates the data accepted signal, bringing the system back to its initial state.

The source unit does not send the next data item until the destination unit indicates that it is ready by disabling the data accepted signal. Data in serial transmission can be sent using either a synchronous or asynchronous method

- **Synchronous Serial Transmission:** Both the sender and receiver operate using a shared clock signal, ensuring that data bits are transmitted at a fixed rate dictated by the clock pulses.
- **Asynchronous Serial Transmission:** Unlike the synchronous method, this approach does not rely on a shared clock signal. Instead, it uses special bits at the beginning and end of each character to manage data transmission. This method is commonly used in interactive terminals.

Structure of an Asynchronous Serial Transmission

Each character in an asynchronous transmission consists of three key components:

1. **Start Bit:** A single bit set to 0, signaling the beginning of a new character.
2. **Character Bits:** The actual data representing the character.
3. **Stop Bit(s):** One or more bits set to 1, indicating the end of the character transmission.
    - When no data is being transmitted, the communication line remains in a high (1) state.
    - When the sender is ready to transmit, it sends the start bit (0) to indicate the beginning of a new character.
    - After transmitting the character bits, the stop bit (1) ensures that the receiver properly detects the end of the transmission.

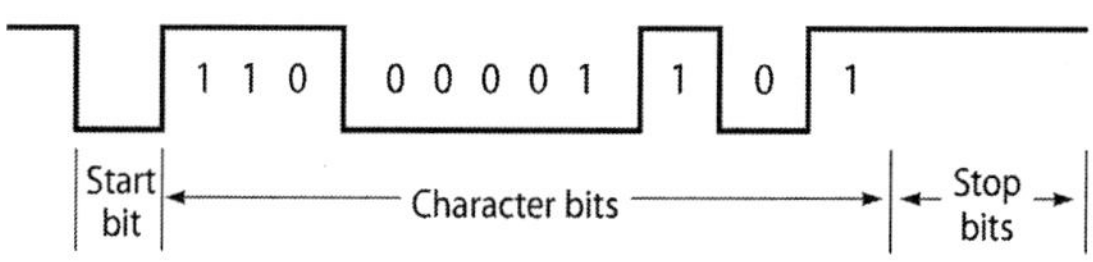

Fig 4.3: Asynchronous serial transfers

Asynchronous Serial Transmission: UART

A Universal Asynchronous Receiver-Transmitter (UART) is a specialized integrated circuit designed to facilitate communication between a computer and external interactive terminals. It serves as an asynchronous communication interface, ensuring smooth data exchange without requiring a shared clock signal.

Baud Rate

The baud rate refers to the speed at which serial data is transmitted, measured in bits per second (bps). It determines how fast data travels between the sender and receiver in an asynchronous communication system.

FIFO Buffer (First-In, First-Out Buffer)

A FIFO (First-In, First-Out) buffer is a type of memory unit that temporarily stores data while maintaining the order in which it was received.

Key Features of a FIFO Buffer

- The first data item to enter the buffer is also the first to exit, ensuring sequential processing.
- It has separate input and output terminals, allowing data to be stored and retrieved at different rates.
- The stored data remains in the same order as it was received, ensuring accuracy.
- FIFO buffers are particularly useful in asynchronous data transfer, helping manage data flow efficiently when sender and receiver operate at different speeds.

4.3 Modes of Transfer

Data transfer to and from peripherals may be handled in one of the three modes

1. Programmed I/O
2. Interrupt initiated I/O
3. Direct memory access

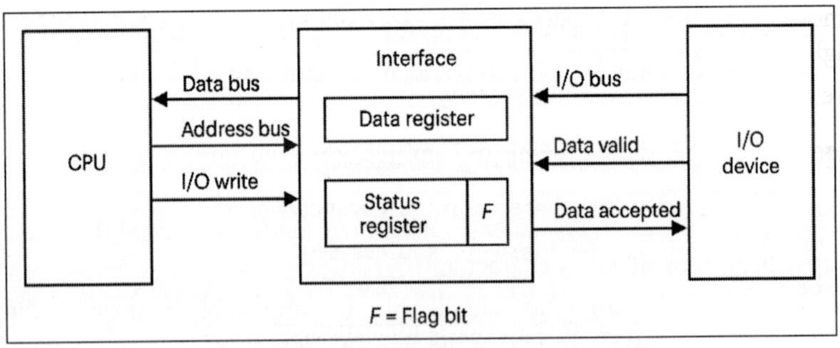

Fig 4.4: Data transfer from I/O device to CPU

1. Programmed I/O

- Each data transfer operation is initiated by an instruction in the program.
- Data is exchanged between a CPU register and a peripheral device.
- The CPU continuously monitors the peripheral to check if it is ready for data t.

- The processor remains in a program loop until the I/O unit signals readiness.

This method is inefficient as it keeps the CPU occupied, preventing it from handling o tasks.

2. Interrupt-Initiated I/O

- Instead of the CPU constantly checking the device, the interface monitors the device's status.
- When the device is ready for data transfer, it generates an interrupt request to notify the CPU.
- Upon detecting the interrupt signal, the CPU temporarily pauses its current task, executes a service routine to handle the I/O transfer, and then resumes its previous task.
- This approach reduces CPU workload and enhances efficiency.

3. Direct Memory Access (DMA)

- The DMA controller handles data transfers directly between memory and I/O devices, bypassing the CPU.
- The CPU initiates the transfer by providing the starting memory address and the number of words to be transferred, then resumes executing other tasks.
- When memory access is required, the DMA controller requests memory cycles through the memory bus.
- Upon approval by the memory controller, the DMA directly transfers data into memory.
- During DMA operations, the CPU temporarily pauses its memory access to avoid conflicts, ensuring smooth data transfer.

4.4 Priority Interrupts

Multiple I/O devices can generate interrupts simultaneously. A priority interrupt system determines which device gets serviced first. Devices with higher data transfer speeds are given higher priority over slower ones.

There are two methods to establish priority:

1. Software-Based Priority (Polling Procedure)

- All interrupt requests share a common branch address.
- The system polls the interrupt sources sequentially, checking higher-priority devices first.
- Once the highest-priority device is identified, its service routine executes.
- Disadvantage: If there are many devices, polling can take longer than servicing the interrupt itself, leading to inefficiencies.

2. Hardware-Based Priority System

- A dedicated hardware unit manages interrupt requests and determines their priority.

- Each device has its own interrupt vector, allowing the system to identify the device quickly.
- No polling is required, making it significantly faster than software-based priority management.
- Priority can be established using serial or parallel interrupt connections.

Serial or Daisy-Chaining Priority Interrupt

- In this method, devices are arranged in a priority order, with the highest-priority device placed first.
- When a device needs CPU attention, it sends an interrupt request to the CPU.
- The CPU responds by sending an Interrupt Acknowledge (INTACK) signal, which is received by the first device in the chain through its Priority In (PI) line.
- If the first device initiated the request, it places its Vector Address (VAD) on the bus and blocks further signals by setting its Priority Out (PO) line to 0.
- If the first device did not request an interrupt, it passes the INTACK signal to the next device in the chain by setting its PO line to 1.
- This process continues until the requesting device is identified.
- The device with PI = 1 and PO = 0 is the one that originally sent the interrupt request and will be serviced by the CPU.

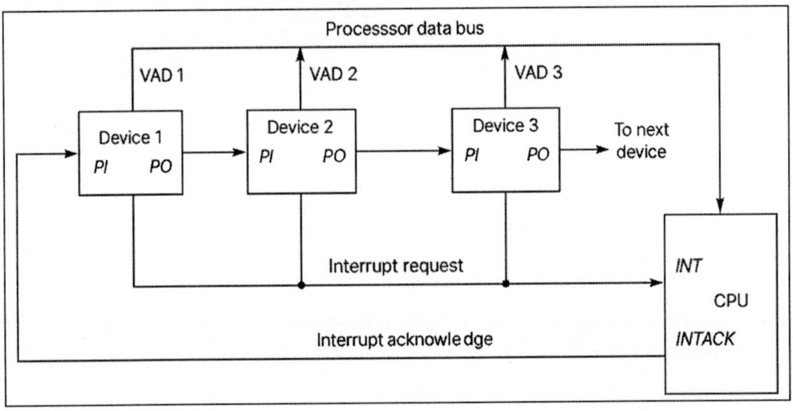

Fig 4.5: *Daisy chain priority interrupt*

1. Parallel Priority Interrupt
2. This method uses an interrupt register, where each bit corresponds to a specific interrupting device.
3. When a device generates an interrupt request, its corresponding bit in the register is set.
4. Priority is determined based on the position of these bits in the register, with higher-priority devices assigned to higher-order bits.
5. A mask register allows control over interrupt handling:
    a. Higher-priority devices can interrupt while a lower-priority device is being serviced.

b. All lower-priority devices can be disabled when a high-priority device is being serviced.

1. The interrupt bit and corresponding mask bit are ANDed and sent to a priority encoder, which determines the highest-priority request.
2. The priority encoder generates vector address bits that direct the CPU to the appropriate interrupt service routine.
3. It also sets the Interrupt Status Flip-Flop (IST) to indicate that an interrupt is in progress.

4.5 I/O Processor (IOP)

- The Intel 8089 is an I/O processor housed in a 40-pin integrated circuit package.
- It features two independent channels that operate separately.
- The IOP is responsible for reading messages from memory, executing operations, and notifying the CPU upon completion.
- It supports 50 basic instructions designed for efficient I/O processing, operating on bits, bytes, or 16-bit words.
- Unlike a general-purpose CPU, its instruction set is tailored for optimized input-output handling.

Functionality & Communication

- The Intel 8089 facilitates efficient data transfers between system components, including I/O to memory, memory to memory, and I/O to I/O.
- In an Intel 8086/8089 microcomputer system, the 8086 functions as the CPU, while the 8089 acts as the IOP.
- Both units share a common memory via a bus controller connected to a system bus (Intel's "Multibus").
- The IOP communicates with various interface units through its local bus.
- The CPU signals the IOP by enabling the channel attention line and selects one of its two channels using a select line.
- The IOP requests the CPU's attention by generating an interrupt request.

Message-Based Communication

- The CPU and IOP exchange messages by writing them into system memory.
- The CPU prepares a message, then signals the IOP via the channel attention line.
- The IOP reads the message, executes the necessary I/O functions, and runs the appropriate channel program.
- Once the operation is completed, the IOP generates an interrupt request to notify the CPU.

Block-Based Communication Scheme

- Communication is structured in blocks, each containing:
  - Control and parameter information
  - An address pointer to the next block

- During initialization, the IOP channels receive the address of the control block.
- A busy flag indicates whether the IOP is currently processing or ready for a new task.
- The CPU issues a Channel Command Word (CCW) to specify the type of operation required from the IOP.

4.6 Direct Memory Access (DMA)

Direct Memory Access (DMA) is a feature in computer systems that allows certain hardware components to access the system's main memory (RAM) independently of the Central Processing Unit (CPU).

Why is DMA Important?

Without DMA, the CPU must handle all read and write operations using programmed input/output (PIO), which keeps it fully occupied during the entire data transfer. This means the CPU is unavailable for other tasks until the operation is complete.

1. The CPU initiates the transfer.
2. The DMA controller handles the data transfer while the CPU performs other tasks.
3. Once the transfer is completed, the DMA controller sends an interrupt to notify the CPU.

The CPU cannot keep up with high-speed data transfers. The system needs to perform useful computations while waiting for a slow I/O transfer.

Where is DMA Used?

DMA is widely used in various hardware systems, including:

- Disk drive controllers
- Graphics cards
- Network cards
- Sound cards
- Multi-core processors (for intra-chip data transfers)

Advantages of DMA

- **Reduces CPU overhead:** Systems with DMA channels can transfer data between devices without heavily involving the CPU.
- **Parallel Processing:** In multi-core processors, DMA allows processing units to transfer data without occupying CPU cycles, enabling computation and data transfer to occur simultaneously.
- **Efficient Memory Operations:**
  - DMA can also be used for memory-to-memory data transfers, reducing CPU workload for large-scale copying or scatter-gather operations.
  - An example of this is I/O Acceleration Technology, which optimizes data movement for high-performance computing.

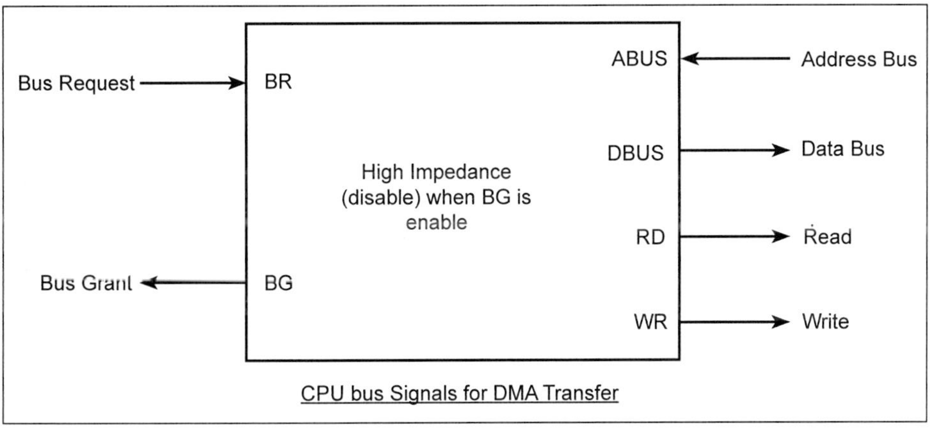

Fig 4.6: *Illustration of DMA transfer*

Burst Mode (Block Transfer Mode)

In burst mode, an entire block of data is transferred in a single, continuous sequence. Once the DMA controller gains control of the system bus from the CPU, it completes the entire data transfer before releasing the bus back to the CPU.

While this method allows for fast and efficient data movement, it temporarily halts CPU operations, rendering it inactive for a longer duration. This mode is also known as "Block Transfer Mode" and is useful for preventing unnecessary data transmission.

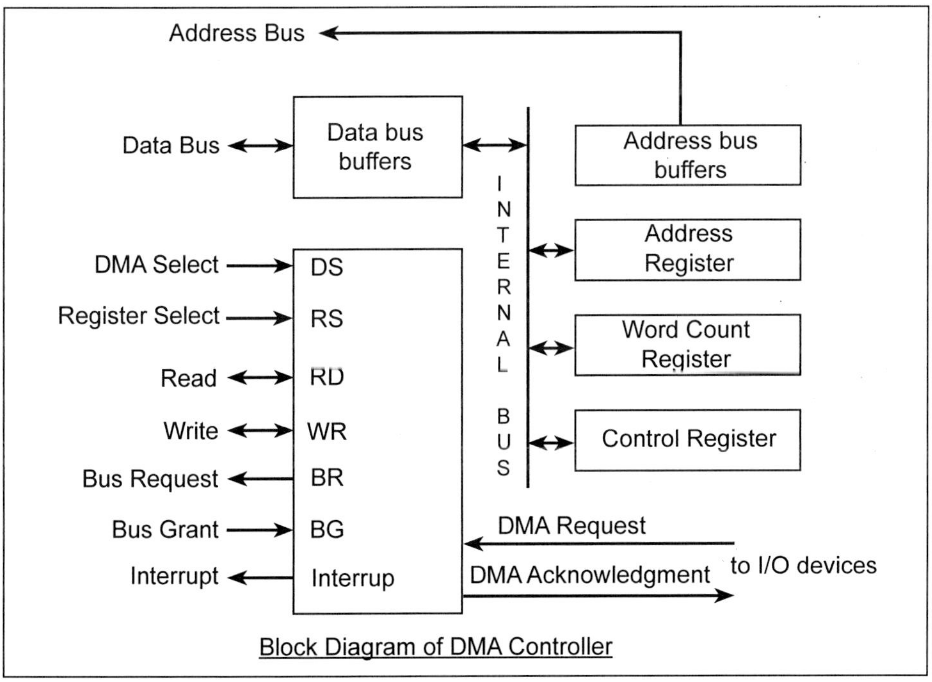

Fig 4.7: *Block diagram DMA Controller*

DMA Transfer Modes

Cycle Stealing Mode

Cycle stealing mode is designed for systems where the CPU cannot be completely disabled for extended periods, as in burst mode. In this mode, the DMA controller gains access to the system bus using Bus Request (BR) and Bus Grant (BG) signals—similar to burst mode. However, instead of transferring an entire block of data at once, the DMA controller transfers one byte at a time before releasing control of the system bus back to the CPU.

This process repeats until the entire block of data is transferred. By alternating between CPU instructions and DMA transfers, cycle stealing allows both CPU processing and data transfer to occur interleaved. While this mode is slower than burst mode, it ensures that the CPU remains active and is not completely halted for long durations. This makes it particularly useful in real-time data monitoring applications.

Transparent Mode

Transparent mode takes the longest time to transfer a data block, but it is the most efficient in terms of overall system performance. Here, the DMA controller transfers data only when the CPU is idle and not using the system buses.

The key advantage of transparent mode is that the CPU never stops executing instructions, making the DMA transfer effectively "free" in terms of CPU time. However, the main challenge is the hardware complexity required to detect CPU inactivity and determine the right time for data transfer.

4.7 Serial Communication

Serial data transmission occurs in three different modes:

1. Simplex Mode
   - Data flows in only one direction.
   - **Example:** Radio and TV broadcasting
2. Half-Duplex Mode
   - Data can be transmitted in both directions, but only one direction at a time.
   - **Example:** Modem communication
3. Full-Duplex Mode
   - Data can be sent and received simultaneously in both directions.
   - **Example:** A two-wire communication circuit

Message Formation and Control Characters

Message transmission involves the use of various control characters to ensure proper formatting and communication between devices. Each character, including these control characters, is sent serially as an 8-bit binary code. This code consists of the 7-bit ASCII representation of the character, with an odd parity bit added as the most significant bit to ensure error detection.

To maintain synchronization between the transmitter and receiver, special SYS characters are used. The message heading begins with the Start of Header (SOH) character, followed by two additional characters that indicate the destination terminal's address.

Bit-Oriented Protocol

In a bit-oriented communication protocol, data is structured into frames, each beginning with an 8-bit flag represented by 01111110. This flag helps both the sender and receiver recognize the start of a new frame.

- Following the flag, the address and control sequence specifies the recipient and the type of operation.
- A Frame Check Sequence (FCS), implemented using a Cyclic Redundancy Check (CRC), is included to detect any transmission errors.
- The ending flag signals to the receiver that the last 16 bits of the frame contain CRC error-checking data.

After the ending flag, the next part of the transmission can be:

- A new frame,
- Another flag, or
- A sequence of consecutive 1's (indicating idle transmission).

To accommodate essential fields like address, control, and frame check, a frame must contain a minimum of 32 bits between flags.

Summary

Input-output organization focuses on how data moves between the CPU, memory, and peripheral devices. Peripheral devices, such as input units (keyboards, mice), output units (printers, displays), and storage devices (hard drives, magnetic tapes), connect to the processor through I/O interfaces. These interfaces handle communication challenges due to differences in data transfer speeds and formats. Computers use either memory-mapped or isolated I/O to address peripherals, ensuring seamless data exchange. I/O buses and interface modules manage multiple devices through commands like control, status, and data transfer operations.

Data transfer methods play a key role in system efficiency. Programmed I/O requires the CPU to manage all transfers actively, making it inefficient for high-speed communication. Interrupt-driven I/O improves performance by allowing devices to notify the CPU only when needed. Direct memory access (DMA) further enhances efficiency by enabling peripherals to transfer data directly to memory without CPU intervention. Priority interrupts determine which device gets CPU attention first, using either software polling or hardware-based prioritization methods like daisy-chaining and parallel priority interrupts. The I/O processor (IOP) offloads processing tasks from the CPU, improving overall performance. Serial communication enables data transfer over long distances using protocols such as UART, synchronous and asynchronous transmission, and bit-oriented communication.

EXERCISES

S.No.	16 Marks Questions	Level
1	Discuss how DMA and interrupt-driven I/O can be balanced in a system to optimize data transfer and CPU utilization. What criteria should be used to decide which method to use for specific tasks?	L4
2	Analyze how each I/O type can be optimized for a system with both high-speed and slower peripherals. How should the system be designed to allocate the most suitable transfer mode to each device type for optimal performance?	L4
3	Explain the I/O interface design for an embedded system that communicates with multiple sensors and actuators. Identify and analyze the protocols involved, and evaluate how they facilitate communication between the CPU and these devices.	L2
4	Compare the different modes of data transfer (programmed I/O, interrupt-driven I/O, DMA) in a data acquisition system. Assess the effectiveness of each mode, and justify which mode would be most suitable for your specific system requirements and why.	L4
5	Discuss the management of priority interrupts in a real-time operating system where tasks have varying priorities. Analyze the methods used for prioritizing and handling multiple interrupt requests, and evaluate their effectiveness in ensuring timely task execution.	L4
6	Explain how implementing DMA can improve the performance of a data-intensive application that frequently accesses disk storage. Describe the role of the DMA controller in enhancing data transfer efficiency, and apply this knowledge to a practical scenario.	L2
7	Discuss the role of an Input/Output Processor (IOP) in offloading processing tasks from the main CPU to enhance system performance. Analyze its advantages and evaluate how it interacts with the main CPU and peripheral devices in your system design.	L4
8	Explain the implementation of serial communication protocols in a distributed sensor network designed for efficient data transmission. Consider factors such as speed, error detection, and data integrity, and apply these considerations to your system design.	L3

S.No.	2 Marks Questions	Level
1	A device needs to transfer the data without CPU intervention. Name two different modes of data transfer that allow this scenario	L2
2	In a multi device system, data consistency is critical. What mechanism can help to ensure the data consistency during transfers?	L2
3	Describe how an I/O interface facilitates communication between the CPU and peripheral devices.	L1
4	How would you choose the appropriate mode of transfer for a real-time system?	L1
5	Differentiate between input and output peripheral devices.	L2
6	Analyze the advantages and disadvantages of using direct memory access (DMA) versus programmed I/O.	L4

S.No.	2 Marks Questions	Level
7	What is the impact of error detection in a serial communication system?	L1
8	If a system uses the First-In-First-Out (FIFO) replacement policy, how would it handle a situation where the cache is full, and a new block of data needs to be loaded?	L2
9	An application frequently reads from a hard drive. How does DMA improve the efficiency of this process?	L2
10	Evaluate the methods for handling I/O requests. List out the disadvantages of using polling over interrupts.	L4
11	Identify a common protocol used for serial communication in a system that interacts with multiple sensors and explain its significance.	L4
12	State one advantage of serial communication over parallel communication when deciding on a method for your project, and briefly explain why this advantage is important.	L2
13	Describe the role of the bus in connecting peripheral devices to the CPU in a new computer system.	L2
14	Explain the purpose of interrupt handling in a computer system that needs to respond quickly to external events.	L3
15	Discuss the role of buffering in data transfer for a system processing large amounts of data.	L2
16	What mechanism can help ensure data consistency during transfers in a multi-device system? Explain how it works.	L1

Characteristics of Multiprocessors

5

UNIT

RATIONALE

Multiprocessor systems play a crucial role in enhancing computational performance, fault tolerance, and system throughput by allowing multiple processors to work together. Understanding interconnection structures is vital for designing efficient data exchange pathways between processors and memory units. Interprocessor arbitration ensures fair and efficient access to shared resources, preventing bottlenecks in multiprocessor environments. Effective communication and synchronization mechanisms enable processors to coordinate tasks efficiently and avoid conflicts when accessing shared data. Cache coherence is critical in maintaining data consistency across multiple caches to ensure correct program execution. Mastering these concepts is essential for designing scalable, high-performance computing systems.

OUTCOMES

This unit introduces multiprocessor architectures, interconnection structures, synchronization mechanisms, and cache coherence strategies. It also discusses arbitration techniques and performance considerations. By the end of this unit, students will:

- Understand different interconnection structures used in multiprocessor systems.
- Learn the significance of interprocessor arbitration in resource allocation and conflict resolution.
- Analyze various interprocessor communication techniques & synchronization methods.
- Study cache coherence problems and strategies for maintaining data consistency.
- Evaluate the benefits and challenges of multiprocessor architectures.
- Compare different synchronization mechanisms used in parallel processing environments.

5.1 Interconnection Structures

Multiprocessor systems are computer architectures that use two or more processors to execute tasks simultaneously. These systems aim to increase computational speed, provide fault tolerance, and improve system throughput. To understand multiprocessor systems in depth, it is essential to study their interconnection structures, arbitration mechanisms, communication and synchronization methods, and cache coherence protocols.

Interconnection structures are the physical and logical arrangements that determine how processors, memory modules, and I/O devices communicate in a multiprocessor system. The performance and scalability of a multiprocessor system heavily depend on the efficiency of its interconnection network.

Classification of Interconnection Structures

1. Time-Shared Common Bus

- All processors share a single communication bus to interact with memory and I/O devices.
- Only one data transfer can occur at a time, which may lead to congestion.
- Suitable for a small number of processors.

2. Multiport Memory

- Each memory module has multiple ports to allow simultaneous access by multiple processors.
- Enhances parallelism but increases hardware complexity and cost.

3. Crossbar Switch

- Provides a dedicated path between each processor and each memory module.
- Composed of a grid of switches that can dynamically connect inputs to outputs.
- Highly efficient but expensive due to the number of switches required.

4. Multistage Interconnection Networks (MINs)

- Use a series of stages with switching elements to connect processors to memory modules.
- Examples include Omega Network, Butterfly Network, and Clos Network.
- Offer a compromise between cost and performance.

5. Hypercube and Mesh Networks

- Processors are connected in multidimensional configurations.
- **Hypercube**: Each processor is a node in an n-dimensional cube.
- **Mesh**: Processors are connected in a 2D or 3D grid.
- Scalable and efficient for distributed memory systems.

5.2 Interprocessor Arbitration

In a multiprocessor system, several processors may request access to a shared resource, such as memory or a communication bus. Interprocessor arbitration is the process of deciding which processor gets access to the resource at any given time.

Arbitration Techniques

1. Serial Arbitration (Daisy-Chaining)

- Processors are connected in a linear sequence.
- A grant signal is passed along the chain; the first processor in the chain has the highest priority.
- Simple but introduces unfairness and potential starvation of lower-priority processors.

2. Parallel Arbitration

- Uses a central arbitration circuit.
- All processors simultaneously send requests; the circuit uses priority logic to grant access.
- Faster and more equitable than daisy-chaining, but requires complex hardware.

3. Dynamic Arbitration

- Priorities are not fixed and may change based on time, usage patterns, or a round robin policy.
- Ensures fairness and efficient resource utilization.

4. Centralized vs. Distributed Arbitration

- **Centralized Arbitration**: A single arbiter (controller) manages all access requests.
- **Distributed Arbitration**: Arbitration logic is embedded within each processor, and processors negotiate access collaboratively.

Key Requirements for Arbitration

- **Fairness**: Equal opportunity for all processors.
- **Efficiency**: Minimal delay in granting access.
- **Scalability**: Support for an increasing number of processors.

5.3 Interprocessor Communication and Synchronization

In multiprocessor systems, interprocessor communication and synchronization are crucial for coordinating tasks and ensuring data consistency.

Interprocessor Communication

1. Shared Memory Communication

- Processors communicate by reading and writing to common memory locations.
- Efficient but requires synchronization mechanisms to avoid conflicts.

2. Message Passing

- Processors send and receive messages explicitly.
- Common in distributed systems where processors have private memory.

3. Memory-Mapped I/O

- Communication with I/O devices through designated memory addresses.
- Used in both uniprocessor and multiprocessor systems.

5.4 Interprocessor Synchronization

Synchronization ensures that processes execute in a well-defined order to maintain consistency in shared resources.

Synchronization Mechanisms

1. Locks and Mutexes

- Provide mutual exclusion to prevent concurrent access to critical sections.
- Must be carefully implemented to avoid deadlocks.

2. Semaphores

- Integer variables used to control access to shared resources.
- Support signaling between processes (e.g., wait and signal operations).

3. Barriers

- Synchronization points where all processes must arrive before any can proceed.
- Useful in parallel computations where processes must complete a phase before moving on.

4. Spinlocks

- A processor continuously checks a lock variable until it becomes free.
- Effective for short wait times but consumes processor cycles.

5. Atomic Operations

- Low-level operations that are executed without interruption.
- Examples: **Test-and-Set, Compare-and-Swap, Fetch-and-Add**.

5.5 Cache Coherence

In multiprocessor systems with individual caches for each processor, maintaining **cache coherence** is essential to ensure that all processors have a consistent view of memory.

Problems in Cache Coherence

1. Inconsistent Views

- Different processors may have stale data if they rely on outdated cache copies.

2. Write Propagation

- Changes made by one processor must be visible to others.

3. Transaction Serialization

- The system must preserve the correct order of memory operations across processors.

Cache Coherence Protocols

1. Directory-Based Protocols

- A central directory keeps track of which caches hold copies of a data block.
- When a processor modifies a block, the directory ensures other caches are updated or invalidated.

2. Snooping Protocols

- All caches monitor (or snoop on) a common bus to detect changes in shared data.
- Most effective in bus-based systems.

Snooping Methods

Write-Invalidate

- When a processor writes to a block, other caches invalidate their copies.
- Ensures only one valid copy exists.

Write-Update

- A processor broadcasts the new value to other caches upon a write.
- All caches update their values simultaneously.

MESI Protocol (Modified, Exclusive, Shared, Invalid)

A widely used snooping-based cache coherence protocol.

- **Modified (M):** Cache holds the only valid copy, and it has been modified.
- **Exclusive (E):** Cache holds the only valid copy, unmodified.
- **Shared (S):** Cache holds a valid copy, and other caches may also have it.
- **Invalid (I):** Cache block is invalid and cannot be used.

Goals of Cache Coherence Mechanisms

- Ensure data consistency across caches.
- Minimize performance overhead.
- Maintain correctness in concurrent execution.

Summary

Interconnection structures define how processors communicate with memory and I/O devices. These include time-shared buses, multiport memory, crossbar switches, multistage networks, and mesh and hypercube topologies, each offering trade-offs in cost, scalability, and performance. Efficient interprocessor arbitration is necessary to manage resource access when multiple processors request shared memory or bus access. Arbitration techniques include serial arbitration, parallel arbitration, and dynamic arbitration, ensuring fairness and minimizing delays. Centralized and distributed arbitration methods determine whether a single controller or all processors collectively manage access control.

Interprocessor communication can be achieved using shared memory or message passing, with synchronization mechanisms such as locks, semaphores, barriers, and atomic operations ensuring orderly execution and preventing race conditions. Cache coherence is essential in multiprocessor systems with individual caches, preventing outdated or inconsistent data from being used. Snooping and directory-based protocols help maintain coherence, with strategies like write-invalidate and write-update ensuring data consistency. The MESI protocol classifies cache states to manage data sharing efficiently. Understanding these concepts allows for the design of high-performance multiprocessor architectures that balance computational speed, efficiency, and data consistency.

EXERCISES

S.No.	16 Marks Questions	Level
1	Evaluate the effectiveness of different cache coherence protocols in maintaining data consistency in a multiprocessor environment. Which protocol would be most suitable for high-performance systems, and why?	L5
2	In a system with four processors accessing a single shared memory module, explain how different interconnection structures could manage this access. Compare a bus-based and a crossbar architecture, focusing on latency, bandwidth, and contention management.	L3
3	Develop a synchronization mechanism for a scenario where two processors are performing parallel tasks with interdependencies on data. Describe how you would use semaphores or mutexes to prevent race conditions while ensuring each processor completes its tasks efficiently.	L6
4	Define multiprocessors and describe the various interconnection structures used in multiprocessor systems. How do these structures influence data flow between processors?	L4
5	Design a cache coherence protocol for a system where multiple processors need access to shared data frequently. Describe the protocol's core mechanisms (e.g., write-invalidate or write-update) and justify how your design minimizes coherence traffic and maintains data consistency across caches.	L6
6	Design an interconnection network for a multiprocessor system in a real-time embedded application where low latency and high reliability are critical. Choose an appropriate interconnection structure (e.g., mesh, crossbar, multistage) and explain your design decisions. Describe how your design addresses data transfer, latency, and fault tolerance	L6
7	Design an interconnection structure for a large-scale data processing system that requires low latency and high bandwidth. Describe the type of network chosen (e.g., crossbar, multistage, bus) and explain how your design addresses the key requirements for speed, cost, and scalability."	L6
8	In a shared-memory multiprocessor system, explain how a write-invalidate protocol would maintain cache coherence if two processors frequently read and write to the same shared data. Discuss the trade-offs of this protocol, particularly focusing on coherence traffic and latency.	L3

S.No.	2 Marks Questions	Level
1	In a scenario where multiple processors need to access the same memory module, describe how a multistage interconnection network could help manage this.	L2
2	List two types of interconnection structures commonly used in computer architecture.	L2
3	Consider a scenario where Processor A and Processor B both need simultaneous access to a single memory module. How could a crossbar switch resolve this conflict?	L2
4	In a system with three processors attempting to access a shared resource, describe how priority-based arbitration would resolve potential conflicts.	L2

S.No.	2 Marks Questions	Level
5	Given a scenario where a processor is stalled due to network congestion, analyze how a bus-based interconnection might affect system performance.	L1
6	Consider a system where two processors perform a parallel task. Describe how barrier synchronization ensures task completion before proceeding.	L3
7	Consider two processors that need to work together on a shared task but at different stages. How could barrier synchronization ensure they only proceed once both have reached a certain point?	L1
8	If Processor A writes new data to a shared variable, how would the 'write-back' approach handle cache coherence differently than 'write-through'?	L2
9	Why might a multistage network be preferred over a bus-based interconnection in high-performance systems?	L2
10	If a real-time application is running on a system with multiple processors, why might fixed-priority arbitration be preferred over round-robin?	L2
11	Why is synchronization necessary for interprocessor communication in shared-memory systems?	L2
12	List two protocols used to maintain cache coherence in multiprocessor systems.	L1
13	Name two methods used for resolving conflicts in interprocessor arbitration.	L2
14	How does round-robin arbitration work in the context of interprocessor communication?	L1
15	Why might a priority-based arbitration method be preferred in real-time systems?	L1
16	State one reason cache coherence is essential in multiprocessor systems	L2